Biological Terrorism

& Weapons

of Mass Destruction

IDEAS in CONFLICT

Gary E. McCuen

GEM
GARY McCUEN
publications inc.

411 Mallalieu Drive
Hudson, Wisconsin 54016
Phone (715) 386-7113

Illustration and Photo Credits

Steve Benson 135; Jim Borgman 29; Matt Davies 53; Robert Gorrell 140; Joe Heller 84; Joel Pett 152; Steve Sack 41; Bill Schorr 67; Mike Shelton 117; Richard Wright 11, 111.

© 1999 by Gary E. McCuen Publications, Inc.
411 Mallalieu Drive, Hudson, Wisconsin 54016

(715) 386-7113

International Standard Book Number
0-86596-177-8
Printed in the United States of America

CONTENTS

Ideas in Conflict

Chapter 3   **CHEMICAL AND NUCLEAR TERRORISM**

Chapter 4 WEAPONS OF MASS DESTRUCTION: IDEAS IN CONFLICT

REASONING SKILL DEVELOPMENT

These activities may be used as individualized study guides for students in libraries and resource centers or as discussion catalysts in small group and classroom discussions.

IDEAS
in CONFLICT

This series features ideas in conflict on political, social, and moral issues. It presents counterpoints, debates, opinions, commentary, and analysis for use in libraries and classrooms. Each title in the series uses one or more of the following basic elements:

Introductions that present an issue overview giving historic background and/or a description of the controversy.

Counterpoints and debates carefully chosen from publications, books, and position papers on the political right and left to help librarians and teachers respond to requests that treatment of public issues be fair and balanced.

Symposiums and forums that go beyond debates that can polarize and oversimplify. These present commentary from across the political spectrum that reflect how complex issues attract many shades of opinion.

A global emphasis with foreign perspectives and surveys on various moral questions and political issues that will help readers to place subject matter in a less culture-bound and ethnocentric frame of reference. In an ever-shrinking and interdependent world, understanding and cooperation are essential. Many issues are global in nature and can be effectively dealt with only by common efforts and international understanding.

Reasoning skill study guides and discussion activities provide ready-made tools for helping with critical reading and evaluation of content. The guides and activities deal with one or more of the following:

RECOGNIZING AUTHOR'S POINT OF VIEW

INTERPRETING EDITORIAL CARTOONS

VALUES IN CONFLICT

WHAT IS EDITORIAL BIAS?

WHAT IS SEX BIAS?

WHAT IS POLITICAL BIAS?

WHAT IS ETHNOCENTRIC BIAS?

WHAT IS RACE BIAS?

WHAT IS RELIGIOUS BIAS?

*From across **the political spectrum** varied sources are presented for research projects and classroom discussions. Diverse opinions in the series come from magazines, newspapers, syndicated columnists, books, political speeches, foreign nations, and position papers by corporations and nonprofit institutions.*

About the Editor

The late Gary E. McCuen was an editor and publisher of anthologies for libraries and discussion materials for schools and colleges. His publications have specialized in social, moral and political conflict. They include books, pamphlets, cassettes, tabloids, filmstrips and simulation games, most of them created from his many years of experience in teaching and educational publishing.

CHAPTER 1

TERRORISM AND WEAPONS OF MASS DESTRUCTION: AN OVERVIEW

RELIGION, IDEOLOGY AND TERROR

James K. Campbell

James K. Campbell, U.S. Navy, testified before two Senate Subcommittees on nuclear, biological, and chemical terrorism in his capacity as a private citizen. He is the author of the recently published book Weapons of Mass Destruction Terrorism.

■ POINTS TO CONSIDER

1. Define "post-modern" terrorism.

2. What are the two reasons the author cites for the emergence of post-modern terrorism?

3. According to the author, what types of groups are prone to using Weapons of Mass Destruction (WMD) in terrorist acts? Describe the groups and discuss why you agree or disagree with the author's assessments.

4. Examine the author's statements concerning terrorists' use of WMD and the effectiveness of legal deterrents. Comment.

Excerpted from the testimony of James K. Campbell before the Subcommittee on Technology, Terrorism and Government Information of the U.S. Senate Judiciary Committee and Senate Select Committee on Intelligence, April 22, 1998.

The traditional, "constrained" terrorist of the twentieth century is supplanted by the ultra-violent "post-modern terrorist" of the twenty-first century.

The ultra-violent act followed by silence is increasingly frequent. Many times in recent years terrorist acts have been committed without a group stepping forward to claim credit for the event. The bombing of Pan Am and the Air India flights; the 1996 bombing of U.S. personnel at Khobar Towers in Dhahran, Saudi Arabia; and the bombing of the Olympic Park Pavilion in Atlanta, Georgia, are prime examples of this phenomenon. This non-verbalization suggests a shift in terms of the message the terrorist act is supposed to send. Where traditional "secular-political" terrorists use the event to gain access to a "bullypulpit" to air their grievances, these "silent terrorists" desire to send a message that creates a superordinary sense of overwhelming fear, and vulnerability amongst their "enemies." Additionally, religious terrorists arguably have no great need for media assistance to articulate their cause as the intended audience is their own closed-cell constituency and God.

This change in the characterization of terrorism may be indicative of a new era, one in which the traditional, "constrained" terrorist of the twentieth century is supplanted by the ultra-violent "post-modern terrorist" of the twenty-first century. These terrorists are post-modern because of the manner in which they employ advanced technology, and anonymity, to conduct ultra-violent acts viewed as disproportionate to those conducted by the "modern terrorists" they are gradually supplanting.

GENESIS OF THE POST-MODERN TERRORIST

The emergence of the post-modern terrorist appears to have two causes. One may be religious revivalism. Religion has played a part in legitimizing ultra-violent acts throughout history, acts which have generally been constrained when perpetrated by the "modern" secular terrorists. Indeed, unscrupulous terrorist leaders with nefarious ideals have oftentimes used religious "veneers" to exploit the faith of the "true believer," manipulating this faith into a weapon of extreme violence that they might perpetuate their own violent agendas. This type of masterful manipulation was evident in Shoko Asahara, leader of the Aum Shinrikyo cult; and the Reverend Jim Jones, leader of "The Peoples' Temple." In 1978, 900 members of Jones's "Peoples' Temple" committed mass

10

Cartoon by Richard Wright.

suicide at the cult's facilities in Jonestown, Guyana.

The second cause is arguably related to the removal of constraints imposed by the Cold War, and the subsequent disintegration of a bipolar world order. As a result, disorder has emerged in which the legitimacy of many states is being challenged by increasing calls from sub-national groups for self-determination. Samuel Huntington affirms this trend in a recent essay wherein he argues that the cause of future conflict will be rooted in a clash of non-state, trans-national cultures. He suggests that ethnic and religious underpinnings will play key roles in supplanting traditional political ideologies with cultural ones. Where these movements cross each other, catastrophic, violent events can erupt. Prime examples of this phenomenon can already be seen in Somalia, Egypt, Sudan, Rwanda, Chechnya, the Balkans, and Indonesia.

TO CAUSE MASS CASUALTIES

Is there a specific type of terrorist group that possesses a "ripeness" to employ Weapons of Mass Destruction (WMD) in order to cause mass casualties? My research conclusions suggest that the type of terrorist group most likely to employ WMD is one which follows a radical religiously oriented ideology. This disposition is heightened when the group incorporates racist or ethnic hate as part of their belief structure. Religiously oriented terrorists

11

are searching for far more than the ability to change perceived flaws in the socio-political order of the state. Their aim: the total destruction of the existing order, supplanting it with a new one of their own design. Cases examined for my study included the Tokyo nerve agent attack committed by members of the terrorist cult Aum Shinrikyo; the bombing of the World Trade Center conducted by a group of *ad hoc,* trans-national Islamic radicals; and a case involving a group of violent white supremacists living in the United States. These cases were analyzed and balanced against an assessment of the Provisional Irish Republican Army (PIRA). While PIRA is similar in many respects to the other three, I believe it unlikely that this group would engage in the use of WMD to cause mass casualties.

My research identified eleven key variables that, when present, provide the necessary and sufficient conditions for a terrorist group to threaten use of WMD to cause mass casualties. A brief description of each key variable follows.

KEY INDICATOR

An ideology is a comprehensive system of concepts and beliefs held by an individual or group. It is an organization of opinions, attitudes and values that determine how we think about society and ourselves.

The ideologies of terrorist groups which manifest a ripeness for WMD use, follow radical religious beliefs, affiliated with apocalyptic millennialism, radicalized redemption, or racist/ethnic hate. Destruction is part of the logic of religion. Every religious tradition carries with it images of chaos and terror. Some forms of religion seem to propel the faithful to militant confrontations. In an essay on "The Logic of Religious Violence," Mark Juergensmeyer identifies several key points that elucidate why religiously oriented ideologies can be dangerous to the extreme.

- Religion domesticates violence. Most histories of religion focus on the struggle between good and evil. Through the ages this struggle has been associated with horrific slaughters conducted against, or on the behalf of, the faithful. Religious stories, myths and symbols (swords, crosses and the like) make religiously oriented killing palatable, even if those acts are ultra-violent.

- Violence sanctioned by religion breaks the state monopoly on morally sanctioned killing and provides the perpetrators with a sense of political independence. It places them on the moral high ground above the state because God's judgment is giving them the "green light" to kill in his name.

APOCALYPTIC MILLENNIALISM/RELIGIOUS IMPERATIVE

The ideology of apocalyptic millennialism is rooted in a belief that the present age of the world is irredeemably evil ruled by a satanic figure personifying evil. This ideology professes a belief that the evil age will soon be ended, destroyed by God (or God's servant), who is good. The subsequent age to follow this event is lauded as one of utopia, where everything is perfect and only those who were formerly oppressed or those who are "true believers" will survive to enjoy it.

A redemptive religious imperative is based on a belief that God will reward his people only when certain prerequisites are fulfilled.

ETHNIC HATE IMPERATIVE

What is meant by a racist or ethnic hate imperative? The definition of the word "racism" in its basic form means to discriminate based on the belief that some races are by nature supreme. The same could be said for the concept of "ethnic hate." Winston Churchill voiced a concern that with the downfall of several dynastic regimes following the conclusion of World War I, the world would see an eruption of inter- and intra-state conflict based in ethnic prejudices. In its most radical state, race and ethnicity are used as a banner cry for prescriptions of terrorist violence and separatism. Witness the mass genocides in Rwanda and the Balkans in the early 1990s, and the Holocaust wherein six million Jews were executed by Hitler's Nazi apparatus. Here in the United States a growing movement of neo-Nazism and white supremacist groups operating under a loosely organized web of militia organizations and revisionist Christian movements may very well pose a threat that could result in the use of WMD. In 1985, members of a racist hate group known as "The Covenant, Sword, Arm of the Lord" (CSAL) were arrested on charges of sedition. The U.S. Justice Department raid on their compound resulted in the discovery of a cyanide-producing laboratory and massive quantities of cyanide stockpiled for the express purpose of poisoning the water supply of an unnamed city.

PUBLIC BACKLASH

For the terrorist group operating under a radical religious imperative, backlash possesses little deterrent value as death holds its own reward for the martyred, while perpetuating the struggle for the living by giving them heroes to avenge and emulate. In fact, backlash may reinforce the resolve of these groups to use WMD, viewing themselves as a closed cell surrounded by forces of evil who ultimately desire to destroy them. Violence to these terrorists is seen as an end in itself whereby the corrupt system of "out-group others" must be totally destroyed or substantially damaged so as to allow, minimally, a negotiated settlement favorable to the group: this to occur even at the risk of the terrorist group being reduced to an ineffective force in the process. As a result, WMD use becomes a rationale choice for the closed cell terrorist group.

READING

2

HATE GROUPS AND TERRORISM

Brian Levin

Brian Levin is associate director for Legal Affairs of the Southern Poverty Law Center's Klanwatch Project. For nearly 20 years, Klanwatch has monitored every major hate group in the United States. The Southern Poverty Law Center is headquartered in Montgomery, Alabama.

■ POINTS TO CONSIDER

1. Examine the statement, "The United States faces a new threat of domestic terrorism unlike any we have previously faced."

2. Why does the author highlight white supremacy groups?

3. Describe "ricin." Explain Levin's concerns about ricin.

4. Compare the Aum Shinrikyo cult and anti-government groups in the U.S., according to the author.

Excerpted from the testimony of Brian Levin before the U.S. Senate Permanent Subcommittee on Investigations, March 27, 1996.

The threat of domestic terrorism committed by anti-government terrorists utilizing weapons of mass destruction (WMD) is a significant one.

We at the Center believe that the United States faces a new threat of domestic terrorism unlike any we have previously faced. Suspected anti-government extremists have attacked police officers, plotted to blow up federal buildings, established armed compounds, and gathered military weapons. So-called "common law" courts are threatening public officials with violence if they carry out their official duties. In the summer of 1995, anti-government extremists from the Tri-State Militia banded together to endorse a war against the United States government. Our intelligence uncovered counter-intelligence networks established by hate groups and anti-government militias targeting public officials, civil rights groups, and the media. In November 1995, federal authorities arrested several people for plotting to blow up several buildings, including our headquarters. Recently, we have identified 809 anti-government Patriot groups, including 441 paramilitary groups operating in all 50 states. At least 47 of those groups have ties to white supremacists. Clearly, this is a movement replete with zealots who embrace violence as the preferred means for establishing their anti-democratic ideals.

SEEKING WMD

There has been a disturbing series of incidents that indicate that patriot extremists have embraced the use of chemical weapons and pathogens as their newest and most dangerous destructive tool.

In November 1995, Aryan Nations member Larry Harris pleaded guilty to possession of freeze-dried bacteria he had illegally obtained from a commercial laboratory for $240. A search of his residence netted hand grenades, homemade explosives and detonating fuses.

In late 1995, four members of the anti-government Minnesota Patriots Council were convicted in federal court for conspiracy to use ricin, a deadly toxin, to kill federal agents and government workers. Ricin, a derivative of the castor bean, is one of the most dangerous toxins known. After inhalation or ingestion, ricin kills by invading human cells and interfering with protein synthesis. The would-be assassins, who joked about spreading the "govern-

16

ment flu," had enough ricin to kill 1400 people. The defendants had learned to make the poison from a mail-order terrorist training manual popular with the Patriot movement.

NOT JUST CASTOR BEANS

In another incident in December 1995, Thomas Lewis Lavy, 54, an army veteran and reputed survivalist, was arrested after thirty federal agents along with U.S. Army biological warfare experts raided the Arkansas farm where he was staying. Agents retrieved 130 grams of ricin (enough to kill 30,000 people), castor beans and three books that detailed how to make ricin and disseminate the poison. Lavy, who said he possessed the mass quantity of poison to kill coyotes, hung himself in his jail cell three days after his arrest.

In 1993 Lavy had been arrested by Canadian custom agents who caught him at a border crossing in possession of four guns, 20,000 rounds of ammunition, $89,000 in cash, a bag of ricin, neo-Nazi material and two books – *The Poisoner's Handbook* and *Silent Death*. These books instruct readers on how to produce deadly toxins. FBI officials believe that Lavy was going to use the money and ricin to fund and arm an underground terrorist militia.

DRAWING CONNECTIONS

Perhaps the starkest example of the threat posed by anti-government ideologues using chemical or biological weapons is the sarin gas attack in the Tokyo subway by the Aum Shinrikyo cult. This attack, which killed twelve and left five thousand injured, represented the first time chemical weapons were used in peacetime by terrorists.

Important similarities exist between this cult and anti-government extremists here. First, like their American counterparts, the Aum Shinrikyo cult promoted wild conspiracy theories, apocalyptic fervor and hatred against their government. Second, the use of chemical and biological toxins as weapons was actively promoted within the movement. Third, the perpetrators intentionally selected their target because the location would likely result in casualties to government officials. The subway station chosen for the attack serviced the main area of the capital where most of the offices of the Japanese government are located.

THE NEWEST WEAPON

While ricin may be the newest toxic weapon of mass destruction in the arsenal of domestic anti-government terrorists, it is not the first toxin considered for use by domestic terrorists. A terrorist plot to poison municipal water supplies was alleged in a 1988 federal sedition indictment of a consortium of white supremacists. The white supremacists were alleged to have been plotting a race war against the United States government. While an all-white jury acquitted the group of sedition charges, the indictment pointed to a coordinated terrorist effort that included toxins as a weapon of choice. The indictment mentioned the group's plans to poison water supplies and their possession of large quantities of cyanide.

Because of our concern over the involvement of white supremacist leaders in the anti-government militia movement and the movement's potential for violence, the Law Center's founder, Morris Dees, wrote to Attorney General Reno and the Attorneys General of six states to alert them to the growing anti-government militia movement. We have subsequently written to every state Attorney General requesting that they enforce their laws against unsanctioned private armies or sponsor such legislation in their states.

SIGNIFICANT THREAT

Today, we wish to convey a similar message: The threat of domestic terrorism committed by anti-government terrorists utilizing weapons of mass destruction, including explosives, chemical toxins and biologic pathogens is a significant one.

THE GLOBAL MENACE OF ORGANIZED CRIME

Benjamin Gilman and Arnaud de Borchgrave

Benjamin Gilman is a Republican representing the 20th district of New York State in the U.S. House of Representatives. He chairs the Committee on International Relations. Arnaud de Borchgrave is the project director of the Global Organized Crime Project for the Center for Strategic and International Studies (CSIS).

■ **POINTS TO CONSIDER**

1. Why does Representative Gilman fear organized crime?

2. Discuss the evidence de Borchgrave presents for Russia's plunder.

3. Compare and contrast American business practice of the late nineteenth century with that of Russian organized crime today.

4. Define "cyberterrorism" and explain why the author highlights it.

Excerpted from the testimonies of Benjamin Gilman and Arnaud de Borchgrave before the U.S. House of Representatives Committee on International Relations, October 1, 1997.

STATEMENT OF BENJAMIN GILMAN:

About two-thirds of the Russian economy is under the sway of organized crime (OC), including 40% of private business, 60% of remaining state-owned enterprises and more than half of the country's 1,740 banks.

Until recently, most of us have viewed the problems of drug-trafficking, organized crime and terrorism as issues of obvious concern, really only of a marginal nature. In other words, drugs were only a danger to a very small percentage of our citizens – or that organized crime was a menace but restricted to car theft, gambling scams and racketeering in big cities. And, finally, that terrorist groups, while dangerous, were usually operating in foreign countries and could only muster up an occasional suicide bomber.

CHOKE-HOLD

All of these groups are far more sophisticated and disciplined than previously suspected. Drug cartels have the ability to move literally hundreds of billions of dollars in and out of legitimate financial systems.

In Colombia, for example, a few years ago, several arrested members of the Medellin Cartel reportedly offered to pay off the Colombian national debt if only their government would not honor its extradition treaty with the United States (which had been honored since 1885). Today the Colombian Constitution has been amended and no longer permits extradition of Colombian nationals.

Organized crime groups, particularly in Russia, now have an almost complete choke-hold on the country's vast natural resources as well as the banks and media. Russia has been described as a "kleptocracy" from top-to-bottom, a semi-criminal state. And there are now terrorist groups, including those sponsored by Iran and Iraq, which are actively recruiting top nuclear scientists in their efforts to obtain nuclear weapons.

NEW CHALLENGES

This new globalized crime wave will take complete advantage

of new technologies to hide their activities and, when combined with their ability to move huge sums of money instantly, actually threaten every free society's ability to assert financial control over its own economy.

These new global cartels could ultimately be capable of buying entire governments and commercial trade zones in emerging democracies and, eventually, undermining established western markets and stable world financial commercial trading systems.

Last but not least, their ability to obtain and hide the purchase of stolen weapons, including nuclear devices, will give any major crime cartel or terrorist organization the necessary means to assert itself through the use of force and intimidation, something we all know is part and parcel of their natural behavior.

STATEMENT OF ARNAUD DE BORCHGRAVE:

Russia's Deputy Military Prosecutor, Lt. Gen. Stanislav Gaveto, captured the crime crisis well when he said Russia is faced with "the wholesale criminalization of the life of our entire society; every pore of the state mechanism is steeped in corruption and abuse..."

About two-thirds of the Russian economy is under the sway of organized crime (OC), including 40% of private business, 60% of remaining state-owned enterprises and more than half of the country's 1,740 banks. Those are estimates of Russia's Interior Ministry. Crime syndicates enjoy the protection of the ruling oligarchy which consolidated its power during Mr. Yeltsin's illnesses in 1996 and early 1997.

GLOBAL CONGLOMERATES

Two hundred of Russia's largest crime gangs are now global conglomerates. There are some 280 on-going criminal investigations of Russian organized crime involvement with U.S. counterparts.

Former First Deputy Minister of the Economy Vladimir Panskov recently wrote in Pravda that $250 billion "leaked from Russia over four years." The Bank of France estimates that in 1994, Russians invested $50 billion in 30 western countries. Interior Minister Kulikov's own estimates range from $150 billion to $300 billion. By way of comparison, total western aid to Russia from all western countries, principally Germany, and from international institutions since 1992 is $74 billion.

"KRYSHA"

The rule of law has been displaced by criminals and gang chieftains who are *de facto* adjudicators: "krysha," or "roof," are the protection rackets that have replaced legal functions and safeguards.

The first round of privatizations supervised by Anatoly Chubais, now a First Deputy Prime Minister, consisted of rigged auctions in favor of pre-selected individuals or banks, with crime syndicates the principal beneficiaries. The Analytical Center of the Russian Academy of Sciences estimated that "55% of the capital and 80% of voting shares were transferred during the privatization process into the hands of domestic and foreign criminal capital." Prosecutor General Yuri Skuratov reported 2,000 privatization crimes in 1996 alone. His military counterpart said he had 6,000 major cases of corruption in the military last year, most of them committed by officers.

The Center for Strategic and International Studies (CSIS) report, the second in a series of seven under the Center's Global Organized Crime Project, dispels the widely held perception that Russia is a market economy run by a hot team of reformers. Many have argued that Russia's struggle against OC and corruption is the primitive accumulation stage of early capitalism, much like the American "robber barons" of the late 19th century.

NOT SELF-CORRECTING

A World Bank report says this is a dangerous assumption that does not hold up to critical analysis. America's early entrepreneurs rode roughshod over laws and created huge industrial enterprises that were of enormous value to society as a whole. Profits were ploughed back in the U.S., not sent abroad for safekeeping in anonymous bank accounts.

In the U.S., a self-correcting political and legal system curbed the excesses of the robber barons and capitalism matured.

In Russia, former Communist Party officials, KGB operatives, and OC syndicate chiefs sold off state assets, did not create new ones, and moved scores of billions of dollars of plunder abroad, instead of reinvesting in Russia.

According to knowledgeable intelligence sources in several countries (U.S., Russia, the U.K. and Germany), the plunder began in early 1986 during the *glasnost/perestroika* phase of the Gorbachev regime. That is when certain key figures of the Communist Party's Central Committee concluded that omnipotence could soon turn to oblivion. So they began advanced planning for the redistribution of the funds and resources of the Soviet Union. These plans included transferring what was then under the control of the Property Section of the Central Committee (CC) – the entire wealth of the country – to new commercial structures outside the control of whatever followed *glasnost* and *perestroika* policies.

BRINGING "THE ROOF" DOWN

On the economic front, the battles that lie ahead are for tax reform, breaking up the monopolies, establishing transparency in commercial practices and improving corporate governance. For any of these battles to be won, a reliable enforcement and regulatory regime must be created to replace the "krysha," and other forms of private intimidation and extortion as the means for settling business disputes. Interior Minister Kulikov estimates that one third of business expenses go to bribing officials. His Interior Ministry issued a 30-page report which says, "The main conclusion of criminologists and economists who compiled the report was that the state of law and order in the area of organized crime offers no ground for optimism."

Russian OC operates with criminal counterparts in some 50 foreign countries. Law enforcement is faced with a new breed of trans-national criminals with high-tech methodologies. The scope for large-scale international fraud to flourish undetected grows in tandem with the power and speed of computers, which now doubles every nine months.

CYBERTERRORISM

The coming wave of cyberterrorism will present an even greater challenge. New, highly educated, computer literate generations of terrorists are not thinking in terms of truckloads of explosives, nor briefcases of sarin gas, nor dynamite strapped to the bodies of fanatics, as Hamas and Islamic Jihad do today. Tomorrow's high-tech terrorists are plotting attacks with one's and zero's, at a place where we are most vulnerable – namely the point at which the "physical" and the "virtual" worlds converge, the place where we live and function and the place in which computer programs function and data moves.

The National Information Infrastructure (NII) is extremely vulnerable to disruption from either physical or logical attack. This insecurity has created what the Department of Defense (DOD) calls "a tunnel of vulnerability previously unrealized in the history of conflict."

Would-be terrorists have been experimenting with the "Net." They clearly perceive a global reach for their activities as they train themselves with the tools of information warfare. In January 1997, the Defense Science Board's Task Force on Information Warfare issued a little-noted report that called for "extraordinary action" because "current practices and assumptions are ingredients in a recipe for a national security disaster." It predicted that by 2005, attacks on U.S. information systems by terrorist groups, international crime syndicates and foreign espionage agencies would be "widespread."

The CIA treats information warfare as one of the two main threats to national security — the other being nuclear, biological and chemical (NBC) weapons of mass destruction. The myth persists that we have not been invaded since 1812. Yet cyberattacks are now a daily occurrence. The fact is that four out of five of our major corporations have been successfully intruded upon — but only 17% of them admit in confidential surveys that they have alerted law enforcement agencies. First, they do not wish to undermine consumer confidence and shareholder value by exposing themselves to possible leaks, and second, they believe there is little law enforcement can do about it, given its meager resources.

"BIG TIME" PAYOFF

Foreign espionage agencies, including some of allied countries, have used hacker networks brazenly to overcome triple electronic firewalls and sniff out proprietary secrets from some of our high-tech firms. Today there are already eight hostile or potentially hostile nations that have developed the required technology and skills to wage information warfare by means of electronic

LOOSE NUKES

Stories about the exploits of a "nuclear mafia" are a staple of the tabloid press, and mainstream publications speculate that politically motivated terrorists or international crime syndicates could resort to nuclear blackmail to threaten Western industrial nations....

In 1993, Germany recorded 234 incidents of suspected smuggling of an assortment of nuclear-related materials. Then, with the seizure of 300 grams of plutonium at the Munich airport in August 1994, it appeared that – for the first time – there was solid evidence that weapon-grade material was coming on the market....

Nonetheless, little meaningful analysis of the risk of nuclear terrorism has been undertaken. This discrepancy may result in part from the fact that nuclear terrorism falls into a "high risk-low probability" category – it is a risk whose consequences are serious but whose probability must be rated very low....

Karl-Heinz Kamp. "An Overrated Nightmare." **Bulletin of Atomic Scientists.** July/August 1996.

sabotage and lethal destruction, and 120 nations have developed computer attack capabilities.

Meanwhile, cybercrime pays – big time. The Chaos Computer Club (CCC), a German hackers group based in Hamburg, demonstrated on national TV that they can use Microsoft Internet technology to steal money from one account and put it into another without the use of a personal ID or PIN number during an online banking transaction.

Law enforcement's capabilities are now from five to ten years behind the trans-national crime curve. Its agencies should be given authorization to order state-of-the-art computer systems as soon as they become available, thus bypassing the 49 months it now takes to order, acquire and install a new system (v. nine months in the private sector).

4

A PUBLIC HEALTH RESPONSE TO TERRORISM

Michael Osterholm, Ph.D., M.P.H., and Luther L. Fincher, Jr.

Michael Osterholm, Ph.D., M.P.H., is State Epidemiologist and Chief of Acute Epidemiology Section for the Minnesota Department of Health. He is also adjunct professor in the Division of Epidemiology at the University of Minnesota School of Public Health. His testimony on the domestic response to bioterrorism was delivered on behalf of the American Society for Microbiology. Luther L. Fincher, Jr., is Chief of the Charlotte, North Carolina, Fire Department. He delivered his testimony on strengthening the local response to domestic terrorism in his capacity as Second Vice President of the International Association of Fire Chiefs.

■ POINTS TO CONSIDER

1. Why does Osterholm differentiate biological weapons from other weapons of mass destruction?

2. Discuss reasons for increased vulnerability to biological attack in the U.S. What does he recommend to strengthen the domestic response to biological terrorism?

3. Contrast "crisis" and "consequence" management of terrorism. Upon which method do the authors focus?

4. Why does Fincher place his emphasis on local responses to terrorism? How does he suggest improving local responses?

Excerpted from the testimonies of Michael Osterholm and Luther L. Fincher, Jr., before the Subcommittee on Labor, Health and Human Services, Education and Related Agencies of the U.S. Senate Committee on Appropriations, June 2, 1998.

STATEMENT OF MICHAEL OSTERHOLM

Initial detection of a bioterrorist attack could be difficult, and the response to it would certainly entail a complex strategy.

Biological weapons differ in several important respects from other weapons of mass destruction and thus require a different approach for deterrence, detection, and response. Understanding these differences is critical to formulating public policy.

A key difference is that most biological weapons cause diseases that exist in nature and may occur spontaneously in human populations. Therefore, the first and most fundamental defense strategy for dealing with bioterrorism is to develop effective means for combating all infectious diseases. Fears about state-sponsored or individual terrorists intentionally spreading agents of infectious disease should not distract us from the underlying war against naturally occurring diseases, including emerging infections that threaten to spread as new epidemic waves causing illness and death.

IMPROVED PUBLIC HEALTH INFRASTRUCTURE

Improving the public health infrastructure and biomedical research capacity is the most effective approach for addressing both familiar and new or emerging infectious diseases. However, several expert committees, including one convened by the Institute of Medicine, have concluded that the ability of the U.S. public health system and allied health professionals to deal with emerging diseases is in serious jeopardy. For example, a 1992 survey by the Council of State and Territorial Epidemiologists indicates that the number of professional positions dedicated to infectious disease surveillance in most states has fallen below a vital threshold, making infectious disease surveillance efforts inadequate throughout much of the United States. Even with the recent infusion of federal support for the emerging infections program, the overall infrastructure for infectious disease surveillance at the state and local level has suffered. In part this has been due to the substantial reductions in support for surveillance of vaccine-preventable diseases, HIV infection and tuberculosis. Frequently, state and local health departments will share infrastructure support with other disease programs. In many states no one is tracking foodborne and waterborne diseases any longer. Such gaps in surveillance have a direct impact on our overall ability to respond to threats or acts of bioterrorism.

COMPLEX IDENTIFICATION AND RESPONSE

Such deficiencies count for a great deal because, unlike nuclear or conventional bombs or even chemical weapons, a biological weapon is unlikely to cause instant harm. Thus, because symptoms take time to develop, an act of bioterrorism may go undetected for days or even weeks after it occurs. If the disease were even moderately contagious, secondary cases would occur among contacts of ill persons and would also be randomly distributed. Delay in detecting these cases by hours could mean the difference between an order of magnitude in the increased number of serious illnesses and deaths. In particular, for such agents as anthrax, plague and even smallpox, a delay of hours in responding to these potential disease problems will result in many more cases and deaths.

Thus, initial detection of a bioterrorist attack could be difficult, and the response to it would certainly entail a much more complex strategy than is typically required following an incident involving explosives or chemical weapons. Current systems for counteracting bioterrorist attacks are erroneously being built on models for incidents involving chemical agents, such as the release in 1995 by members of the Aum Shinrikyo of sarin gas in Tokyo. In this and other cases like it, the impact of the attack is immediate, localized, and the affected area and victims are readily identified. Hence, medical management and decontamination efforts can be directed quickly to specific sites. Moreover, first responders and military strike teams can be trained to anticipate such events in a useful fashion, thereby giving some assurance that damages may be minimized, if not altogether avoided.

GENERAL HEALTH CARE COMMUNITY

In the case of a clandestine biological attack, however, sick individuals will not likely be met first by specially trained first response teams. Instead, these infected individuals will seek medical attention in a variety of civilian settings, including emergency rooms, doctors' offices, or clinics at scattered locations. Successful detection of a secret bioterrorist attack thus depends on many members of the health care and public health system promptly

Cartoon by Jim Borgman. Reprinted with permission, **King Feature Syndicate.**

recognizing an unusual infectious disease pattern. This will require the concerted efforts of clinicians, specialized laboratory personnel to confirm the diagnoses of the suspected disease agent, public health experts to determine that multiple cases have occurred simultaneously but unexpectedly, and, finally, additional experts to conclude that the cases of disease in question were not acquired naturally but through a deliberate act of bioterrorism.

STATEMENT OF LUTHER L. FINCHER, JR.:

When an act of terrorism occurs, the local fire and emergency service organizations alone respond immediately to deal with the incident and begin mitigation. Their operations in the first two or three hours will largely determine the number of lives saved and the eventual outcome of the incident. In almost all cases, the federal assets responding to an incident will not arrive until six to eight hours have passed, well after the most critical period. This demonstrates that local first responders are unassisted for the most critical hours.

This is the point at which public health is most vulnerable. The local healthcare system must respond to treat patients while ensuring that first responders and its own workers do not become victims as well.

CONSEQUENCE MANAGEMENT

Federal response plans regarding terrorism usually describe two roles – "crisis management" and "consequence management." Crisis management deals with the enormous task of trying to prevent an incident from occurring. Consequence management concerns with planning for an incident before it occurs, then for recovery and rehabilitation after the event.

Let me point out a third area – the area called "local emergency response" immediately after the event. Local emergency response fits between crisis and consequence management. It begins at the point immediately following notification of the terrorist act. Local emergency response is that intense and vivid period of several hours when local first responders cope with the aftermath of a major incident. It is that time when local first responders work alone.

EQUIPMENT

On the equipment issue, there is a clear and demonstrated need for sophisticated detection equipment. Firefighters need to know what they are facing – what chemical or biological agent. First, this information is necessary to protect ourselves and, second, to determine the correct strategy and tactics to deal with the incident. When such equipment is made available to first responders, provision must be made for training on its use, maintenance, spare parts, and future upgrades. There is also a need to assist local response agencies in acquiring appropriate personal protective equipment. Local fire departments simply do not have the resources to purchase all the protective equipment necessary to deal with a large-scale chemical or biological attack.

Another essential equipment need is the ability to engage in a large-scale decontamination effort. Some federal organizations, such as the Marine Corps' Chemical Biological Response Force, have some decontamination capabilities. However, they can only be effective when pre-positioned in anticipation of a specific event. The effectiveness of the capabilities are greatly diminished when geography dictates a response time of six to eight hours. Therefore, local first responders and public health providers must have policies, procedures, and facilities in place to deal with any nuclear, biological, or chemical agent that may be used.

MORAL PROHIBITION

As more states take up biological weapons, the probability increases that terrorists will do the same. Indeed, Aum Shinrikyo leaders said they were inspired to develop chemical and biological weapons by publicity about Iraq's capabilities at the time of the Gulf War. Thus, as the moral barrier against biological and chemical weapons falls among nations, the likelihood of use by subnational groups increases....

Leonard L. Cole. **The Eleventh Plague: The Politics of Biological and Chemical Warfare.** New York: W.H. Freeman and Company, 1997.

HOSPITAL, RADIO CAPABILITY

In a terrorist incident, the fire and emergency services will be responsible for triage, emergency medical treatment, and transportation of the sick and wounded. A large-scale WMD incident will sorely test even the largest community's ability to deal with mass casualties. Drug and antidote caches, decontamination facilities, and hospital pre-plans must be a focus of congressional inquiry and policy. Veterans Administration Hospitals should be considered for an important role.

In 1996, the Public Safety Wireless Advisory Committee submitted its report to the Federal Communications Commission (FCC). One of its key recommendations was that the FCC set aside 2.5 MHZ of spectrum for inter-operability. We need Congress to push for the policy to direct the FCC to establish several frequency ranges for inter-operability purposes. In the World Trade Center and Oklahoma City incidents, the inability of the first responder agencies to communicate with each other and then with other levels of government severely hampered effective operations. This problem must be corrected.

INTERPRETING EDITORIAL CARTOONS

This activity may be used as an individualized study guide for students in libraries and resource centers or as a discussion catalyst in small group and classroom discussions.

Although cartoons are usually humorous, the main intent of most political cartoonists is not to entertain. Cartoons express serious social comment about important issues. Using graphics and visual arts, the cartoonist expresses opinions and attitudes. By employing an entertaining and often light-hearted visual format, cartoonists may have as much or more impact on national and world issues as editorial and syndicated columnists.

Points to Consider:

1. Examine the cartoon in Reading Four.

2. How would you describe the message of the cartoon? Try to describe the message in one to three sentences.

3. Do you agree with the message expressed in the cartoon? Why or why not?

4. Are any readings in Chapter One in basic agreement with this cartoon?

5. Does the cartoon support the author's point of view in any of the readings in this book? If the answer is yes, be specific about which reading or readings and why.

CHAPTER 2

BIOLOGICAL TERRORISM

BIOLOGICAL WEAPONS: AN HISTORICAL PERSPECTIVE

George W. Christopher, Theodore J. Cieslak, Julie A. Pavlin and Edward M. Eitzen, Jr.

The following piece appeared in the Journal of the American Medical Association (JAMA). JAMA *began publishing in 1883 and today is the most widely read medical journal globally. Among the objectives of the journal are to publish original important and well-documented articles on a diverse range of medical topics and to inform readers about non-clinical aspects of medicine and public health, including the political, philosophic, ethical, legal, environmental, economic, historical and cultural.*

■ POINTS TO CONSIDER

1. Describe some of the earliest known biological weapons employed.

2. What events promoted the contemporary proliferation of biological weapons research?

3. Why did the U.S. give up its biological weapons program in the early 1970s?

4. Discuss the threat of biological terrorism.

Excerpted from Christopher, George W., et al. "Biological Warfare: An Historical Perspective." **Journal of the American Medical Association**, vol. 278, no. 5. August 6, 1997: 412 (6).

These have been used to contaminate wells, reservoirs, and other water sources of armies and civilian populations under attack since antiquity, through the Napoleonic era, and into the 20th century.

Recognition of the potential impact of infectious diseases on armies resulted in the crude use of filth, cadavers, animal carcasses, and contagion as weapons. These have been used to contaminate wells, reservoirs, and other water sources of armies and civilian populations under attack since antiquity, through the Napoleonic era, and into the 20th century. The use of fomites directly against humans has continued, as evidenced by the smearing of pungi sticks with excrement by the Viet Cong in the early 1960s.

EARLY ATTEMPTS

One of the earliest recorded attempts of using fomites against a population illustrates the complex epidemiologic issues raised by biological warfare. During the 14th-century siege of Kaffa (now Feodossia, Ukraine), the attacking Tatar force experienced an epidemic of plague. The Tatars attempted to convert their misfortune into an opportunity by catapulting the cadavers of their deceased into the city to initiate a plague epidemic. An outbreak of plague was followed by the retreat of defending forces and the conquest of Kaffa....Since plague-transmitting fleas leave cadavers to parasitize living hosts, we would suggest that the corpses catapulted over the walls of Kaffa may not have been carrying competent plague vectors.

During the French and Indian War (1754-1767), Sir Jeffrey Amherst, commander of British forces in North America, suggested the deliberate use of smallpox to "reduce" Native American tribes hostile to the British. An outbreak of smallpox at Fort Pitt resulted in the generation of fomites and an opportunity to execute Amherst's plan. On June 24, 1763, Captain Ecuyer, one of Amherst's subordinates, gave blankets and a handkerchief from the smallpox hospital to the Native Americans and recorded in his journal, "I hope it will have the desired effect." While this adaptation of the Trojan horse ruse was followed by epidemic smallpox among Native American tribes in the Ohio River Valley, other contacts between colonists and Native Americans may have contributed to these epidemics. Smallpox epidemics among immunologically naive tribes of Native Americans following initial contacts with Europeans had been occurring for more than 200 years. In addition, the transmission of smallpox by fomites was inefficient compared with respiratory droplet transmission....

WORLD WAR WEAPONS

Substantial evidence suggests that Germany developed an ambitious biological warfare program during World War I, featuring covert operations in neutral trading partners of the Allies to infect livestock and contaminate animal feed to be exported to Allied forces....Operations in the United States included attempts to contaminate animal feed and to infect horses intended for export during World War I....

Japan conducted biological weapons research in occupied Manchuria from 1932 until the end of World War II under the direction of Shiro Ishii (1932-1942) and Kitano Misaji (1942-1945). Unit 731, a biological warfare research facility located near the town of Pingfan, was the center of the Japanese biological weapons development program and contained 150 buildings, five satellite camps, and a staff of more than 3000 scientists and technicians. Additional units were located at Mukden, Changchun, and Nanking. Prisoners were infected with pathogens including *B anthracis, Neisseria meningitidis, Shigella spp, Vibrio cholerae,* and *Yersinia pestis.* At least 10,000 prisoners died as a result of experimental infection or execution following experimentation during the Japanese program between 1932 and 1945....

THE U.S. PROGRAM

In the United States, an offensive biological program began in 1942 under the direction of a civilian agency, the War Reserve Service. The program included a research and development facility at Camp Detrick, Maryland (renamed Fort Detrick in 1956), testing sites in MIssissippi and Utah, and a production facility in Terre Haute, Indiana. Experiments were conducted using pathogens, including *B anthracis* and *Brucella suis.* After the war, the production facility was leased and converted to commercial pharmaceutical production. Ishii, Misaji, and other Japanese scientists in American custody who had participated in the Unit 731 program were granted immunity from war crimes prosecution on the condition that they would disclose information obtained during their program. Secret debriefings were conducted during the postwar era....

By the late 1960s, the U.S. military had developed biological bacterial pathogens, toxins, and fungal plant pathogens that could be directed against crops to induce crop failure and famine. In addition, weapons for covert use using cobra venom, saxitoxin, and other toxins were developed for use by the Central Intelligence Agency.... President Nixon terminated the U.S. offensive biological weapons program by executive order in 1969 and 1970.... The Central Intelligence Agency was admonished during a 1975 congressional hearing for illegally retaining samples of toxins after presidential orders mandating their destruction.

While many welcomed the termination of the U.S. offensive program for moral and ethical reasons, the decision to terminate the offensive biological program was motivated by pragmatic considerations....By outlawing biological weapons, the arms race for weapons of mass destruction would be prohibitively expensive, given the expense of nuclear programs....

STATE PROGRAMS

An epidemic of anthrax occurred during April 1979 among people who lived and worked within a distance of four km in a narrow zone downwind of a Soviet military microbiology facility in Sverdlovsk (now Ekaterinburg, Russia). In addition, livestock died of anthrax along the extended axis of the epidemic zone out to a distance of 50 km.

The Soviets maintained that the epidemic was caused by ingestion of contaminated meat purchased on the black market. In 1992, Boris Yeltsin, the president of Russia, admitted that the facility had been part of an offensive biological weapons program and that the epidemic had been caused by a nonintentional release of anthrax spores. It was determined that air filters had not been activated early on the morning of April 3, 1979. Inhalation anthrax was identified at autopsy as the cause of death in victims. At least 77 cases and 66 deaths occurred, constituting the largest documented epidemic of inhalation anthrax in history....

Information regarding the Iraqi offensive biological program was obtained after the Persian Gulf War during UN weapons inspections. Iraqi officials admitted to having had an offensive biological weapons program that included basic research on *B anthracis*, rotavirus, camel pox virus, aflatoxin, botulinum toxins, mycotoxins, and an anti-crop agent (wheat cover rust). Fortunately, biological weapons were not used during the Persian Gulf War. The Iraqi government claims to have destroyed its biological arsenal after the war. Research and production facilities that had escaped destruction during the war were demolished by the UN Special Commission on Iraq (UNSCOM) in 1996. The Persian Gulf War and postwar findings have led to a recent decision by the U.S. military to develop a plan to immunize troops against anthrax.

TERRORISM

The biological threat posed by non-state-sponsored terrorists was demonstrated by the intentional contamination of salad bars in Oregon restaurants with *Salmonella typhimurium* by the Rajneeshee cult during late September 1984. This incident resulted in 751 cases of enteritis and 45 hospitalizations. Although the Rajneeshees were suspected, and despite rigorous epidemiologic analyses by the Wasco-Sherman Public Health Department, the Oregon State Health Division, and the Centers for Disease Control, the origin of the epidemic as a deliberate biological attack was not confirmed until a cult member admitted to the attack in 1985....

The threat of biological terrorism resurfaced following the Aum Shinrikyo sarin attack of the Tokyo subway system in March 1995. Police raids and investigations of the cult's facilities disclosed evidence of a rudimentary biological weapons program. The cult was allegedly conducting research of *B anthracis, Clostridium botulinum,* and *C burnetii.* The cult's arsenal seized by police allegedly contained botulinum toxin and drone aircraft equipped with spray tanks. The cult had allegedly launched three unsuccessful biological attacks in Japan using *B anthracis* and botulinum toxin and had sent members to the former Zaire during 1992 to obtain Ebola virus for weapons developments.

These incidents underscore the difficulty of differentiating biological attacks from naturally occurring epidemics or endemic disease and emphasize the increased risk of epidemics during hostilities because of deteriorating hygiene, sanitation, and public health infrastructure....

THE NATURE OF BIOLOGICAL TERRORISM

Col. David Franz

Colonel David Franz is the Deputy Commander of the U.S. Army Medical Research and Material Command.

■ POINTS TO CONSIDER

1. Define biological warfare.

2. Contrast biological and chemical weapons.

3. What is the difference, according to the author, between biological warfare and biological terror?

4. Explain the author's view on the likelihood of biological warfare (BW) attack, or the likely form in which an attack would come.

Excerpted from the testimony of Col. David Franz before the U.S. Senate Joint Committee on Judiciary and Intelligence, March 4, 1998.

I believe the biological terrorism threat to our cities is real.

Biological warfare may be defined as the intentional use of microorganisms or toxins to produce death or disease in humans, animals or plants. Microorganisms include bacteria and viruses, which are also sometimes called replicating agents. Such agents can multiply within our bodies and produce disease or death after infection with a relatively small number of organisms. Biological toxins can be thought of as chemicals which are produced not by man, but by other living things – animal, plants or microorganisms. Toxins do not make more of themselves, so the exposure dose itself is what causes illness. What distinguishes biological warfare from biological terrorism? The two differ in breadth – in the number of agents that can be used effectively – and in the potential countermeasures available to deal with each. We have, generally, fewer tools and less information to protect citizens from terrorism than we have to protect a defined military force from the classical biological warfare agents. I should note that, with regard to biological weapons, the threat to the force today may be more like the terrorist threat to our cities than the battlefield scenario for which we prepared during the Cold War.

WAR V. BIOLOGICAL TERRORISM

Before I discuss the more technical aspects of biological warfare and compare it to biological terrorism, I will note several factors that make these biological threats unique – as compared to chemical and nuclear weapons – and explain why these threats are of special concern at this time. Facilities and equipment designed for legitimate applications can be used to produce biological agents; the facilities for Research and Development, scale-up and production of agents, especially on a terrorist scale, are widespread throughout the world to include the United States. This is frequently termed the "dual use" problem. Secondly, the collapse of the former Soviet Union and subsequent reduction in funding of its massive biological warfare infrastructure may have resulted in a vulnerability for recruitment by states trying to establish biological warfare programs. Finally, the incredible advances in biotechnology over the past ten years – which hold great promise of changing our lives and those of our children for the good – can potentially be used for evil, as well. These factors make the important job of our intelligence community extremely difficult and

Cartoon by Steve Sack. Reprinted with permission, **Star Tribune,** Mpls.

complicate effective implementation of nonproliferation efforts.

BIOLOGICAL V. CHEMICAL WEAPONS

Although chemical warfare agents work by completely different mechanisms and are much more toxic – most of them are volatile and active on the skin, like gasoline – biological agents are neither volatile nor dermally active. In a liquid preparation, whether anthrax bacteria or botulinum toxin or Ebola virus, the biological agents will not move from an open container into the air without the addition of energy. We could spill any of these on the floor in this hall, clean it up with disinfectant, and go about our business. Not so for the chemical agents, which would vaporize and make us sick or kill us. Likewise, the majority of biological agents are not dermally active, so just getting them on intact skin will typically not cause disease. Fortunately, those two characteristics make the proliferator's job – or the bioterrorist's job – more difficult. There are significant technical barriers that must be overcome to use biological agents effectively against our armed forces, and because of the factors I have mentioned above less formidable barriers to using them effectively against our society.

Other important differences between biological and chemical agents include the fact that 1) biological agents can be isolated from the environment, 2) some are contagious – therefore, disease

41

could spread from exposed persons to a broader population 3) generally much smaller volumes of biological agent are required for a given target footprint and 4) the period between exposure and onset of clinical signs is typically much longer for biological than for chemical agents. The latter fact makes crisis management, and particularly triage of patients, after an overt biological attack much more difficult than for a chemical attack.

DISSEMINATING DISEASE

Because of the physical characteristics of biological agents, the proliferator can probably expose a large target population efficiently only by generating what we call a "respirable," or breathable aerosol. A respirable aerosol is an airborne cloud of particles that can be inhaled and retained in our respiratory tracts. It would be difficult to produce mass casualties on a modern battlefield through contamination of food or water, even though the oral route is another way that biological agents can effectively enter our bodies. The terrorist who would produce hundreds of thousands of casualties with biological agents would need to develop an aerosol cloud, not just spray material into the air or let it escape from a container as was done with a crude chemical agent in the Tokyo subway. Nevertheless, food and water contamination might be good enough for the terrorist, who may simply want to cause panic or make the nightly news.

COLD WAR ERA

Not all biological agents are created equal. If we examine the agent lists developed by proliferators during the Cold War era, and even before, we see that most programs eventually focused on ten to 15 agents. There is a reason the lists were so small. When one considers the hundreds of infectious agents and toxins, only a small subgroup has the physical and biological properties needed for a mass-casualty producing biological weapon. These characteristics include ease of production, infectivity or toxicity, stability – during processing, storage and in the environment – and, of course, the ability to effectively cause illness or death in the exposed population. Anthrax comes out high on everyone's list because the spore form of the organism is very stable. Some viruses require just a few organisms to infect and are so easy to grow to high concentrations that their relatively poor stability becomes less important. Two of the toxin families have been popular because of their extreme lethality or incapacitation effects. The point is that very few agents have the characteristics that make them good biological warfare, battlefield, mass-casualty weapons agents. However, terrorists don't have to deal with all the technical constraints intrinsic to the objectives of large national biological warfare programs.

PROTECTION FROM ATTACK

That multiplicity of potential terrorist agents makes the job of those charged with protecting our civilian population difficult. To protect a defined military force we can use prophylactic vaccines or drugs, we can place detectors on the battlefield and we can provide full-face respirators which our troops can don with adequate warning of an attack. After the attack, we can use diagnostic tools to identify the agent and possibly the exposed population and treat them with drugs or, in some cases, immunotherapy. We can decontaminate victims, although we believe decontamination is less critical following an aerosol biological attack than it might be following a chemical attack. It is important to note that, with the exception of the protective mask, the decontaminants and a subset of the detectors, the passive countermeasures must be designed for specific agents, or families of agents. Furthermore, in the case of a terrorist attack, we may not be able to use the vaccines, prophylactic drugs, detectors or the physical protection.

Following an announced or at least an overt attack, we may only react to support an already exposed population – a population that, at the time, may look and feel no different than you and I do today. After a covert attack, local health care providers may be the first to notice that it has occurred; the outcome of such an attack may resemble a disease outbreak, compressed in time. It will likely be the relatively few scientists and clinicians in the Department of Defense (DOD) and the Department of Health and Human Services (HHS) who conduct research with these organisms daily, who can provide the technical support to local, state and federal responders, and make the difference between normal life and illness or death for our citizens.

POSSIBLE THREAT, LITTLE PANIC

I think there is some good technical news in this story. I believe that an effective, mass-casualty producing attack on our citizens in this country would require either a fairly large, very technically competent, well-funded terrorist program or state sponsorship. Although it will always be possible to obtain virulent organisms from the environment, the technical hurdles between the agar slant and a cloud covering many square miles of one of our cities are significant. One can quite easily produce a liquid preparation of a number of these agents, but liquids are difficult to disseminate effectively as aerosols. If the terrorist can acquire a good dried material, with a consistency like talcum powder, it would be easier to disseminate effectively. However, most organisms don't like to be dried and the process requires special equipment. Even with the high-quality dry material, weather and wind conditions make dissemination of the agent and the resultant footprint unpredictable.

From my mostly medical research frame of reference, I believe the biological terrorist threat to our cities is real. I am concerned about state-sponsored terrorism, because with help, an individual or small group could truly produce mass casualties. But even following an effective attack, our established public health infrastructure within national, state and local governments could make an enormous difference.

44

READING

7

THE SOVIET BIOLOGICAL WARFARE PROGRAM

Richard Preston

Richard Preston is an author, whose novels include The Hot Zone *and* The Cobra Event. *He spent six years researching and writing about viruses and biological weapons.*

■ **POINTS TO CONSIDER**

1. What is "Biopreparat?"

2. Describe the extent of the biological warfare program of the Former Soviet Union (FSU), according to the author.

3. In light of the break-up of the Soviet Union, why is the author concerned about the biological warfare (BW) program of the Soviets?

Excerpted from the testimony of Richard Preston before the U.S. Senate Select Committee on Intelligence and the Subcommittee on Technology, Terrorism and Government Information of the U.S. Senate Judiciary Committee, April 22, 1998.

At its height in the late 1980s, Biopreparat employed around 32,000 scientists and staff. It was scattered in about fifteen major biowarfare facilities across the Former Soviet Union.

The Soviet biological weapons program was known as "Biopreparat" or "The System" by the scientists who worked in it. Biopreparat was founded in 1974 by a special state directive to carry on with a clandestine bioweapons program, shortly after the Soviet Union signed the Biological Weapons Convention, which bans the development, stockpiling, and use of bioweapons.

BIOPREPARAT

Biopreparat was like an egg. The outside part was devoted to peaceful medical research. The hidden inner part, the yolk, was devoted to the creation and production of sophisticated bioweapons powders – smallpox, black plague, anthrax, tularemia, the Marburg virus, and certain brain viruses.

At its height in the late 1980s, Biopreparat employed around 32,000 scientists and staff. It was scattered in about fifteen major biowarfare facilities across the Former Soviet Union. The sites included a huge virus research facility called Vector, in Siberia. Biopreparat was staffed by scientists, but it was controlled and funded by the Soviet Ministry of Defense. The military was responsible for developing the weapons delivery systems, while Biopreparat made the hot warhead material. The scientists and military people didn't get along with each other, and there was a lot of mutual suspicion and dislike. Biopreparat was an inefficient bureaucracy. It resembled the Soviet space program or the Soviet hydrogen bomb project. The system was flawed, but it had some very definite successes.

GERM DEVELOPMENT

For example, Soviet scientists developed an airborne, powdered form of the Marburg virus – a close cousin of the Ebola virus, which causes people to die by hemorrhage from the openings of the body. The weaponized Marburg virus was reportedly so potent that monkeys (and presumably people) would die after exposure to a single particle trapped in the lungs. They also discovered a way to mass-produce Marburg virus using a simple technology that is available to any country.

The powders were stockpiled by the ton for quick loading into inter-continental ballistic missiles (ICBMs) and special weapons systems. Biopreparat was required to stockpile no less than 20 tons of freeze-dried smallpox powder, which was stored in bunkers near missile launching silos. The smallpox was targeted on the United States. We were a so-called "deep target." This means that since the United States was in a different continent, it was presumed that smallpox would rage in North America but not get back to Russia. The smallpox and other agents were produced to be loaded into special MIRV biological warheads designed to be mounted on ICBMs. Twenty tons of smallpox would fill a large number of strategic biowarheads. The capacity of these biowarheads was roughly 100 pounds of dry smallpox. This implies that the Soviets had perhaps 100 to 400 smallpox warheads. They probably had an equal number of Black Death warheads. The Soviets could have easily hit the 100 largest cities in the United States with devastating combined outbreaks of strategic smallpox and Black Death – an attack that could easily kill as many people as a major nuclear war.

TECHNOLOGY OF DEATH

The biowarhead had special cooling systems to keep a virus alive during the heat of re-entry. It was meant to drop down over a city on a parachute. When the warhead reached a certain height over the ground, it would burst apart, and bomblets full of smallpox would fly off all directions. The bomblets were egg-shaped and made of aluminum, and were about the size of small melons. They would pop open with soft sound, and powdered smallpox (or Marburg, or Black Death) would disperse in the air over the city, almost instantly becoming invisible. The powder was very fine, and was treated with plastics and resins to increase its potency and longevity in the air.

A weaponized bioparticle is very small, about one to five microns across. That's the size that lodges best in the human lung. To get an idea of the size of a weaponized particle, you could think about fifty of them lined up side by side: they'd span the thickness of a human hair. They are invisible in the air, and they can travel for miles. There is a time lag after the release – people have become infected, and now they're incubating the virus – and then people start to die.

EXPORTING KNOWLEDGE

Have scientists left Russia bringing their expertise and master seed strains of smallpox with them, or other bioweapon seed strains? We would be foolish not to presume so. In 1990, about 4,500 scientists and researchers worked at Vektor. Today, only about 1,000 to 1,500 people work there. The rest have gone elsewhere: into other jobs, other labs, or they're unemployed. Some, I do believe, have left Russia. I have been told by American scientists who have visited Vektor that the security around the smallpox storage area is pathetic – "one pimply-faced kid holding a Kalashnikov that may not have any bullets in it," in the words of one American scientist.

This underlines the need for the United States to stockpile the smallpox vaccine. There are currently only seven million usable doses on hand. Experts believe that in any terrorist release of smallpox, even a small one, the virus is so contagious that it would be necessary to vaccinate at least 20 to 30 million Americans to stop the outbreak. The U.S. Army has a new way to make smallpox vaccine very cheaply and in large quantities, but it needs to be tested and approved. Enough smallpox vaccine for every citizen – 270 million doses – could be stored in a small building the size of a garage, and the vaccine would remain potent for decades. By having plenty of vaccine ready, we effectively remove smallpox as a good weapon from the arsenal of a would-be terrorist. It would also take smallpox out of the hands of Saddam Hussein far more effectively (and cheaply) than bombing his laboratories – for the American vaccine could be offered to any country threatened by smallpox, thus making the virus much less credible as a menace or a weapon.

DOUBLESPEAK

To this day, the Russian government and leading Russian biologists have never clearly admitted to the world that they had a large bioweapons program. They have not disclosed its extent or its basic work. They've never owned up to what they did. Instead, to this day, we continue to hear evasions, doublespeak, and outright lies. American experts who've been to Russia and inspected the biowarfare facilities have nagging suspicions that bioweapons research and development still continues in Russia. Biological weapons are an ethical and scientific abomination, a disgrace to biology. Leading American scientists should come out and say so, loudly and clearly. It's time for our scientific leadership to make its voice heard.

Biological weapons are exceedingly dangerous, but some sharp thinking and some wise planning right now can make us much safer.

AUM SHINRIKYO: A GERM WARFARE PROGRAM

Senate Committee on Governmental Affairs Staff

March 12, 1995, twelve passengers died and another 5,000 people were injured in a nerve gas (sarin) release on the Tokyo subway. Members of the obscure Aum Shinrikyo cult released the gas. Investigation of the religious group since the Tokyo subway incident revealed startling evidence of a privately funded germ and chemical warfare program sponsored by Aum Shinrikyo. The following is an examination of the germ warfare program prepared by the Staff for the Senate Committee on Governmental Affairs.

■ **POINTS TO CONSIDER**

1. Give a brief history and description of Aum Shinrikyo.

2. Describe the biological weapons program of the cult. How does the report explain Aum Shinrikyo's desire and ability to develop weapons of mass destruction?

3. In addition to the March 20, 1995, sarin nerve gas attack, does the report indicate the cult made other offensive attempts?

Staff for the Senate Committee on Governmental Affairs. **Global Proliferation of Weapons of Mass Destruction: A Case Study on the Aum Shinrikyo.** Washington, D.C.: U.S. Government Printing Office, 1996.

The Aum cult was aggressively involved in chemical and biological weapons production. Their operations involved chemical and biological research, development and production on a scale not previously identified with a sub-national terrorist group.

The Aum Shinrikyo (Supreme Truth) was founded in 1987 by Shoko Asahara, a 40-year old legally blind former yoga teacher. In 1977 Asahara began the study of yoga and in 1984 he formed a company called the Aum Shinsen-no kai which was a yoga school and publishing house. From various Aum publications it appears that around 1986 he changed his own name to Shoko Asahara and, in 1987, the name of his yoga group to the Aum Shinrikyo – a Sanskrit derivative literally meaning "teaching the universal or supreme truth."

RELIGIOUS RECOGNITION: A TURNING POINT

In August 1989, the Tokyo Metropolitan Government granted the Aum official religious corporation status. This law provided the Aum various privileges including massive tax breaks and *de facto* immunity from official oversight and prosecution.

The Aum Shinrikyo is grounded in Buddhism but with a strong mixture of assorted Eastern and Western mystic beliefs. Aum literature claims that only one person, Shoko Asahara, has attained the highest level of consciousness and exists in the state of Nirvana. Although this concept is widely known in Western religions, "Armageddon" or the "end of the world" is not a normal tenet of Buddhism or other Eastern religions popular in Japan. However, it was a core element of the Aum religion with salvation only coming at the end of Armageddon to those who adopted the Aum faith. Asahara foretold salvation for those Aum members who have attained a higher state through the teachings of the "Supreme Master" – Asahara. Asahara also preached salvation even to those of his members who perished in the predicted Armageddon since they were assured a special status in their reincarnated state.

MEMBERSHIP AND ASSETS

The cult claimed a membership as high as 65,000, the large majority of whom, 30,000 to 50,000, were in Russia. These numbers have not been publicly corroborated by the Japanese government although most of the officials and Aum experts the Staff interviewed placed the worldwide membership in the 40,000 to 60,000 range.

The Aum was very wealthy. Japanese government estimates place its assets at over 100 billion yen or approximately one billion dollars . They list 16 separate pieces of property in 11 different prefectures belonging to the Aum. They also note that the cult possessed a large amount of liquid assets including a large helicopter, boats, gold bars, and cash.

GAS, BUGS, DRUGS AND THUGS

The Aum cult was aggressively involved in chemical and biological weapons production. Although, the extent of their success is not fully known to this date, the Staff found evidence that they successfully produced nerve agents such as sarin, tabun, soman and VX, biological agents such as botulism and anthrax and controlled substances such as LSD.

Their operations involved chemical and biological research, development and production on a scale not previously identified with a sub-national terrorist group. They created a relatively sophisticated chemical and biological research facility without attracting the attention of either Japanese or foreign governments. In the course of these operations, they not only produced potential weapons but also illegal drugs for their own use and for sale to others.

The cult's motivation for the production of chemical and biological weapons is inextricably linked to its Armageddon prophesy. The cult had as a basic belief that there would be a major war between Japan and the United States that would involve weapons of mass destruction.

BIOLOGICAL WEAPONS

Materials seized at the Aum facilities and other evidence confirms that the Aum had embarked upon an intense research and development program for the production of biological weapons. Judging from this evidence, Japanese authorities believe the Aum succeeded in producing botulism toxin. The same Japanese authorities are less certain but have serious concern that the Aum had also produced anthrax bacillus.

Both botulism toxin and anthrax are viewed by experts as

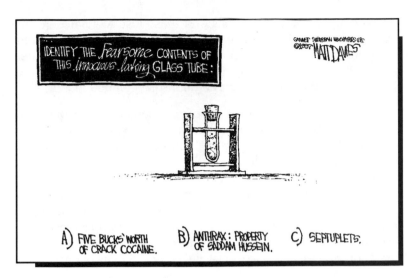

Cartoon by Matt Davies. Reprinted with permission, **UFS.**

serious weapons of mass destruction. In a 1993 report of the Office of Technology Assessment, it is noted that botulism toxin is a poison made by a bacterium, *Clostridium botulinum.* It is one of the most poisonous substances known. The fatal dose of botulin toxin by injection or inhalation is about one nanogram (a billionth of a gram) per kilogram of weight.

Anthrax is the name given for a severe illness caused by the bacterium *Bacillus anthraxis.* It is considered one of the prototypical biological warfare agents. In nature, anthrax is primarily a disease of cattle and sheep but can also infect humans. It can survive for long periods of time in the soil in a dormant state. After infection, it reverts to an active phase in which it multiplies rapidly in the host body and secretes deadly toxins.

After inhalation into the lungs, anthrax spores travel to the lymph nodes of the chest, where they become active, multiplying and releasing three proteins that function as a potent toxin. This toxin results in uncontrollable hemorrhaging and fatal tissue damage. In addition to its lethality anthrax has other characteristics that make it an attractive BW agent, including the ease of production.

CONFESSION, DISCOVERY

The Staff has confirmed that Seiichi Endo, Health and Welfare Minister for the cult, confessed that he had been working on developing biological weapons and was close to finalizing this effort before the Tokyo incident. He claims to have embarked upon this work under the specific directions of Asahara. Other Aum followers have also confessed to their involvement in the biological program at the cult's Kamikuishiki compound.

In the compound, the police have found large amounts of equipment that is indispensable for cultivating bacteria and viruses. Also uncovered were large amounts of "peptone," a substance used to cultivate bacteria, as well as quantities of books and materials on the production of botulism, cholera and dysentery. The amount of peptone seized was phenomenal. Apparently there were 100 to 200 metal drums of peptone seized at the Aum facilities, each having a capacity of 18 liters. By comparison, university research classes are said to typically use only about one liter of peptone per year. Thus, the Aum were expecting to propagate a huge quantity of bacteria.

Subsequent discoveries by the police were equally disturbing. It appears from official Japanese government material reviewed by the Staff that the police determined that Seiichi Endo had produced an antibody for botulinus and was constructing a four-story concrete facility for further development of biological weapons at another Aum site in Naganohara. That facility was to be equipped with a so-called "clean room" with specialized ventilation systems and a sealed room for protecting cultivated bacteria from leaking.

FAILED GERM ATTACKS

Probably the most chilling of all the reports coming out of Japan were those that the Aum had actually attempted to use bacteria warfare. The Staff has learned that a number of devices were found by the Tokyo police that authorities believe may have been intended to disperse anthrax. Three attache cases were discovered on March 15, 1995, five days before the Tokyo gas attack, at the Kasumigaseki subway station in Tokyo. Each contained a small tank holding an unknown liquid, a small motorized fan and a vent and battery. Unfortunately, none of the liquids was recovered for analysis. Experts have told the Staff that these devices were crude dissemination devices for bacterial or chemical agents. Additionally, the Staff has learned from a number of government sources that the cult had obtained at least two radio-controlled drone aircrafts whose likely use was also to distribute biological weapons.

In addition, the Staff has recovered documents from the Aum's attempts to purchase material in the United States that may be relevant to their biological program. The Aum wanted to obtain hundreds of camcorder batteries and small fans as well as thousands of small serum bottles. All are similar to the components used in the attache cases.

The Staff has also learned that the police suspect that the Aum dispersed anthrax bacilli at their Tokyo headquarters. This belief is based upon a confession by one of the former Aum members. The event occurred in June 1993 and coincided with complaints from neighbors of a foul odor. The police report that the Aum's Tokyo headquarters building seemed to have been equipped for bacteria production.

EBOLA

Equally disturbing have been a number of press reports in late May 1995 concerning the Aum's interest in the Ebola virus. The Staff has confirmed that members of the Aum sent a purported medical mission to (the former) Zaire in 1992 to assist in the treatment of Ebola victims. The press reports allege that in actuality the Aum was attempting to find a sample of the Ebola strain to take back to Japan for culturing purposes.

THE BIOLOGICAL WEAPONS CONVENTION: AN OVERVIEW

U.S. Arms Control and Disarmament Agency

Biological and chemical weapons have generally been associated with each other in the public mind, and the extensive use of poison gas in World War I (resulting in over a million casualties and over 100,000 deaths) led to the Geneva Protocol of 1925 prohibiting the use of both poison gas and bacteriological methods in warfare. At the 1932-1937 Disarmament Conference, unsuccessful attempts were made to work out an agreement that would prohibit the production and stockpiling of biological and chemical weapons. During World War II, new and more toxic nerve gases were developed, and research and development was begun on biological weapons. Neither side used such weapons....

In the postwar negotiations on general disarmament, biological and chemical weapons were usually considered together with nuclear and conventional weapons. Both the United States and Soviet Union, in the 1962 sessions of the Eighteen-Nation Disarmament Committee (ENDC), offered plans for general and complete disarmament that included provisions for eliminating chemical and biological weapons.

An issue that long hindered progress was whether chemical and biological weapons should continue to be linked. A British draft

---

"Convention on the Prohibition of Development, Production and Stockpiling of Bacteriological (Biological) and Toxin Weapons and Their Destruction," ed. U.S. Arms Control and Disarmament Agency (ACDA), Washington, D.C., 1996.

convention submitted to the ENDC on July 10, 1969, concentrated on the elimination of biological weapons only. A draft convention proposed in the General Assembly by the Soviet Union and its allies on September 19 dealt with both chemical and biological weapons. The Soviet representative argued that they had been treated together in the Geneva Protocol and in the General Assembly resolutions and report, and should continue to be dealt with in the same instrument. A separate biological weapons convention, he warned, might serve to intensify the chemical arms race.

The United States supported the British position and stressed the difference between the two kinds of weapons. Unlike biological weapons, chemical weapons had actually been used in modern warfare. Many states maintained chemical weapons in their arsenals to deter the use of this type of weapon against them, and to provide a retaliatory capability if deterrence failed. Many of these nations, the United States pointed out, would be reluctant to give up this capability without reliable assurance that other nations were not developing, producing, and stockpiling chemical weapons.

While the United States did not consider the prohibition of one of these classes of weapons less urgent or important than the other, it held that biological weapons presented less intractable problems, and an agreement on banning them should not be delayed until agreement on a reliable prohibition of chemical weapons could be reached.

Shortly after President Nixon took office, he ordered a review of U.S. policy and programs regarding biological and chemical warfare. On November 25, 1969, the President declared that the United States unilaterally renounced first use of lethal or incapacitating chemical agents and weapons and unconditionally renounced all methods of biological warfare. Henceforth the U.S. biological program would be confined to research on strictly defined measures of defense, such as immunization. The Department of Defense was ordered to draw up a plan for the disposal of existing stocks of biological agents and weapons. On February 14, 1970, the White House announced extension of the ban to cover toxins (substances falling between biologicals and chemicals in that they act like chemicals but are ordinarily produced by biological or microbic processes).

The U.S. action was widely welcomed internationally, and the example was followed by others. Canada, Sweden, and the United Kingdom stated that they had no biological weapons and did not intend to produce any. It was generally recognized, however, that unilateral actions could not take the place of a binding, international commitment. A number of nations, including the Soviet Union and its allies, continued to favor a comprehensive agreement covering both chemical and biological weapons.

Discussion throughout 1970 in the General Assembly and the Conference of the Committee on Disarmament (CCD) – as the ENDC was re-named after its enlargement to 26 members in August 1969 – produced no agreement. A breakthrough came on March 30, 1971, however, when the Soviet Union and its allies changed their position and introduced a revised draft convention limited to biological weapons and toxins. It then became possible for the co-chairmen of the CCD – the U.S. and Soviet representatives – to work out an agreed draft, as they had done with the Non-Proliferation and the Seabed Treaties. On August 5, the United States and the Soviet Union submitted separate but identical texts.

On December 16, the General Assembly approved a resolution, adopted by a vote of 110 to 0, commending the convention and expressing hope for the widest possible adherence....

The convention was opened for signature at Washington, London, and Moscow on April 10, 1972. President Nixon submitted it to the Senate on August 10, calling it "the first international agreement since World War II to provide for the actual elimination of an entire class of weapons from the arsenals of nations...."

READING

9

THE BIOLOGICAL WEAPONS CONVENTION: AN INDUSTRIAL PERSPECTIVE

U.S. Pharmaceutical and Biotechnology Industries

The following reading is excerpted from the White Paper on Strengthening the Biological Weapons Convention *(BWC) which represents the industry positions of U.S. Biotechnology and Pharmaceutical Industries. For more information, contact the Biotechnology Industry Organization (BIO) which represents over 700 biotechnology companies, academic institutions and state biotechnology centers involved in the research and development of health care, agriculture and environmental products. BIO, 1625 K Street, NW, Suite 1100, Washington, DC 20006-1064.*

■ POINTS TO CONSIDER

1. Discuss the unique concerns, according to the reading, that the biotechnology industry has with BWC compliance.

2. Explain the industry's position as to the utility of thorough on-site inspections.

3. According to the reading, describe the foreseen consequences of on-site inspections.

4. What does the biotechnology industry believe is the appropriate focus of inspections?

Excerpted from "Implementation of the Biological Weapons Convention: An Industrial Perspective," U.S. Pharmaceutical and Biotechnology Industries' *White Paper on Strengthening the Biological Weapons Convention.*

Experience in Iraq and other countries has demon-strated that intrusive on-site inspections have an extremely low potential (perhaps zero) to discover the manufacture and/or storage of biological agents during an inspection, even on short notice.

The biotechnology and pharmaceutical industries strongly support the strengthening of the 1972 Biological Weapons Convention (BWC). Our industry recognizes the deadly effect of these weapons when used against crops, animals and people. We therefore welcome the opportunity to work with the government to develop a regime for preventing the production and use of biological weapons.

UNIQUE ISSUE

The biotechnology and pharmaceutical industries will be significantly impacted by proposed BWC compliance verification measures. Verification of the BWC raises unique issues compared to either the Nuclear Nonproliferation Treaty or the Chemical Weapons Convention. Small samples of a microorganism can be grown under relatively simple conditions to rapidly produce large volumes of a desired product. Since the strain of microorganism can be virtually the entire "manufacturing facility," strict efforts are taken by industry to assure the protection of proprietary information.

Our industries employ fermentation processes to manufacture a wide variety of products. Antibiotics, protein therapeutics, and vaccines are end-products directly consumed. Others such as fine chemicals and processing enzymes are intermediates used in the manufacture of other consumer products. Common to all these processes is the reliance on proprietary manufacturing processes including the development of improved microbial strains that are used during fermentation....

The sensitivity to loss of proprietary information is much greater in the pharmaceutical and biotechnology industries than in the basic and fine chemical production industries where numerous non-proprietary intermediates and catalysts are often used. Any implementation of a declaration and verification protocol under the BWC must protect proprietary information for the pharmaceutical and biotechnology industries where the U.S. is the undisputed world leader.

DUAL-USE FACILITIES

The biotechnology and pharmaceutical industries recognize the importance of the BWC and support its goals. Current discussions are moving towards developing a set of measures that, if implemented, will address significant concerns about the proliferation of biological weapons. However, total reliance on any set of measures is complicated because of the potential dual-use nature of many fermentation facilities. While no accurate figure exists, the total number of fermentation facilities may easily reach into the thousands if facilities with a batch capacity of greater than 200 liters are considered (200 liter capacity was chosen only to demonstrate that there are numerous facilities of this size and above and is not intended to serve as an indication of the minimum vessel size for agent manufacture). This would include industrial facilities producing biomedical products (antibiotics, vaccines, protein therapeutics), chemicals (ethanol, citric acid), foods (yogurt, yeast), beverages (beer, wine, distilled spirits), along with a large number of industrial and university research and development facilities.

Given the large number of facilities and the potential for dual use, any comprehensive reporting requirement would be problematic. Parties to the Convention that have a large industrial fermentation base will have a difficult time not only identifying but also reporting all such facilities. Furthermore, the ultimate value of such information is questionable. A modestly funded international inspectorate would face a daunting task in assessing the verity of declarations for even a small percentage of the facilities.

A far better approach is to increase efforts undertaken at the Third Review Conference regarding enhancing the Confidence Building Measures. Secondly, uniform procedures for the conduct of short notice visits should be developed for those cases of alleged use of BW by one of the parties to the Convention or in cases of unusual outbreak of disease....

SHORT NOTICE VISITS

Short notice visits can be conducted where there is substantial evidence that an offensive biological agent is being produced in a particular facility or in instances of alleged BW use or unusual outbreaks of disease....

Experience in Iraq and other countries has demonstrated that

61

intrusive on-site inspections have an extremely low potential (perhaps zero) to discover the manufacture and/or storage of biological agents during an inspection, even on short notice. Industry experts cite the following reasons:
1) Biological agents can be disposed of rapidly at all stages.
2) All traces of biological agents can be removed very quickly by sterilization and cleaning.
3) Biological agents can be manufactured in one place and formulated into a weapon(s) at different locations.
4) Biological agents can be produced very rapidly and need not be made until after hostilities are initiated.
5) Biological agents will probably be produced in locations that are impossible to locate.

FALSE SENSE OF SECURITY

Industrial experience would indicate that knowledgeable groups focusing their activities on the manufacture of prohibited biological warfare agents could remove all evidence of prohibited work within the notification time frame of a short notice visit no matter how short the notice, even when inspectors are provided with specific direction from human intelligence sources.

Legally binding short notice visits are therefore most likely to:
a) only hinder the manufacture of offensive biological agents, not prevent it,
b) provide a legal regime to prosecute those who are caught, and
c) provide a false sense of security that a facility is not producing biological weapons if no direct evidence is found.

Short notice visits of U.S. industry are certain to occur. Inspectors conducting these inspections are most likely to have worked with the pharmaceutical or biotech industries.

They will immediately recognize valuable proprietary information and may seek to take advantage of it. They will also recognize it will be difficult or impossible to prove where the information came from. Such information is worth hundreds of millions of dollars to a pharmaceutical/biotechnology company....

OFF-SITE INSPECTION

Off-site measures will provide an immediate indication of the degree of cooperation a facility or country will demonstrate. The biotechnology and pharmaceutical industries recognize and respect the right of inspectors to review any public records and ask the inspected site for explanations. Answers that do not divulge proprietary information (example: annual reports of publicly held companies contain large amounts of financial information but further inquiry as to the cost to produce a given product may be proprietary) will be provided.

The observation of the activity within a facility from above the facility or at the fence line is acceptable. Any country or facility which would not permit this could be highly suspect....

The pharmaceutical and biotechnology industries recognize that off-site measures include environmental samples. These samples could include samples of the air, soil, and water outside the facility boundaries. These samples could provide a preliminary but not conclusive indication as to whether prohibited activities are being conducted on site....

EFFECTIVE ON-SITE MEASURES

On-site measures can provide additional information on the types of activities being conducted at a facility. A realistic inspector will know that all equipment in a suspected facility can be used for legitimate or prohibited activities and that the likelihood of finding prohibited agents on the site within 24 hours of notice of visit is almost non-existent. The inspector should therefore focus on potential inconsistencies from the people who work at the facility and from the facility itself....

READING

10

MAKING THE BIOLOGICAL WEAPONS CONVENTION WORK

The Federation of American Scientists

The Federation of American Scientists (FAS) is a private, nonprofit policy organization which engages in analysis and advocacy for science, technology and public policy. The organization was founded in 1945 as the Federation of Atomic Scientists by members of the Manhattan Project.

■ POINTS TO CONSIDER

1. Explain the Federation of American Scientists' (FAS) position on short-notice inspections.

2. Compare and contrast the "green" and "red light" inspection authorization procedures.

3. What concerns do the biotechnology and pharmaceutical industries have with a "red light" procedure?

4. Discuss the potential costs to industry and the BWC of challenge inspections of facilities.

Federation of American Scientists. "Perspectives on BWC Compliance Regime: Issues Affecting Industry." February 1998. Reprinted by permission.

A central element of a Biological Weapons Convention (BWC) compliance regime is the deterrent effect of short-notice challenge inspections.

A small group of individuals with technical expertise from the U.S. pharmaceutical industry and the Federation of American Scientists (FAS) has met periodically to discuss issues and measures related to strengthening the BWC with a compliance regime. The discussions have resulted in greater understanding on both sides, as well as some new ideas. It would be valuable for governments to promote and participate in give-and-take of this kind with industry and other non-governmental representatives in order to elicit the constructive involvement that is needed on all sides in developing an effective and workable protocol.

This paper reflects the private views of the participants in the meetings and not necessarily those of their organizations or any other group. It contains points of agreement reached at sessions held during the first half of 1997.

DECLARATION CONTENTS

Every effort should be made to minimize or eliminate requirements for confidential information in declarations. Organizations should be willing to give any information that is already in the public domain, in order to establish credibility and cooperation. This includes a considerable amount of relevant information of interest to a compliance regime. The industry participants are concerned, however, that if many types of information are requested, it will be impossible for them to be sure that their declarations are always accurate and complete....

A central element of a BWC compliance regime is the deterrent effect of short-notice challenge inspections. Short-notice inspections could also raise questions and highlight the need for future surveillance of a facility. The notice should be made as short as is practical. Although a modern pharmaceutical facility can be cleaned up in a few hours and most other facilities can likely be cleaned up in eight hours, the shorter the notice the greater the likelihood that a mistake in cleanup will be made. Evidence suggesting non-compliance could take many forms: for example, production records that were not destroyed, equipment and supplies that do not fit the declared use of the facility, or, in a very few instances, evidence of undeclared potential BW agents.

CHALLENGE INSPECTION

A request by a State Party for a challenge inspection should be based on evidence suggesting non-compliance at the facility. The evidence should be submitted with the request to the Director General. A mechanism is needed to discourage challenges based on flimsy evidence. It is not possible to specify in advance, however, the elements of evidence required or to assign weights to different kinds of evidence according to their seriousness, since every case will be different.

Evidence will generally be of two kinds: technical and political. Because of the dual-use nature of most biological capabilities, technical evidence of a BWC violation may not be clear-cut, so will require expert judgment. Since a decision should be reached within 24 hours, it would be important to have a standing Committee of Experts on call to provide technical help to the Director General in examining the evidence, before he gives his opinion to the Executive Council.

Alternatively, the Committee could be called on by, and report to, the Executive Council. There would be a certain advantage, however, in having the Committee report to the Director General before the Executive Council is notified of the inspection request, assuming that confidentiality could be maintained. Depending on the Committee's report, the Director General would then have the opportunity to suggest withdrawal of the request. Stopping the proceedings at this point rather than later would prevent any aspersions on the reputation of the facility in question.

The Committee could provide its input without delaying a challenge inspection. The clock should start when the request for an inspection is made, and the inspectors should prepare and head for their destination. They could be recalled, if necessary. The Committee's deliberations and the Executive Council's decision could be made while the inspection team is en route, with a deadline of 24 hours or less. It is desirable to have the inspectors on site as quickly as is physically possible, in order to optimize the potential for detecting illicit activity.

THE ROLE OF THE EXECUTIVE COUNCIL

Two different types of procedures are under discussion: a "red light" procedure, in which the State Parties on the Executive Council need respond to a request only if they wish to stop an

Cartoon by Bill Schorr. Reprinted with permission, **UFS.**

inspection; and a "green light" procedure, in which the Executive Council must vote within a specified short time to approve an inspection.

Any attempt to reduce the speed and certainty of a challenge inspection will seriously degrade the effectiveness of the regime. The red light procedure (with a large vote required, as in the CWC) is fast and sure, and inaction due to apathy will not prevent an inspection from going forward. The green light procedure can also be fast, but apathy would tend to prevent rather than permit the inspection, thus making it less certain. In the green light procedure, Executive Council members who vote to approve take on a visible responsibility for their action. Consequently, since there may be political reluctance to vote in some cases, a green light procedure will tend to discourage challenge inspections. A red light procedure will tend to be more permissive, particularly if a large number of votes is required to deny a request.

PROCEDURAL CONCERNS

A key concern with the red light procedure, if the number of Executive Council votes needed to prevent an inspection is high, is the possibility that an inspection will proceed even if its basis is unfounded or even frivolous. In terms of public relations and cost to a pharmaceutical or biotechnology company (e.g., stock market reaction to the inspection), an unwarranted inspection could substantially damage the company. Challenge inspections should be used to investigate only well-founded suspicions and should avoid inadvertently punishing institutions that are in full compliance.

The green light procedure better answers the industry concern about unwarranted inspections, because more than one Party would have to demonstrate a belief that an inspection was needed. The question is, how large a vote should be required? Industry would consider a large vote to be safer, but it might be difficult to achieve a large vote to approve because of either apathy or irrelevant political considerations, thereby preventing a requesting Party from satisfying its legitimate concerns.

Perhaps a combination of red and green light procedures could satisfy the different concerns. In its simplest form, a mixed red-green procedure would require a vote by at least X-number of Executive Council members to approve and fewer than Y-number of members to deny, in order for the inspection to proceed. The implications of the procedure depend on the values chosen for X and Y, and are not easy to predict. Nonetheless, it might be possible to select values that would satisfy all concerned.

Another possibility would be to set a quorum and let the majority of those voting to approve or to deny decide whether or not to proceed with a requested inspection. Since either "red" or "green" votes could be cast, this is also a mixed red-green procedure. The problem here is the default decision: if the quorum is not met, what should happen? The industry participants feel that all the Executive Council members should weigh the evidence and vote; if they are not willing to commit themselves and meet the quorum, the inspection should not go forward. On the other hand, defaulting to approve the inspection would preserve the rights of the requesting Party and would serve as an incentive for Parties opposing the request to cast votes; if they do not do so, the inspection should proceed. These two points of view have not yet been reconciled, but some form of mixed red-green procedure holds promise for reaching consensus....

THE COSTS TO INDUSTRY

Industry believes that it will incur real costs, e.g., the cost of training to prepare for inspections, whether or not the facility is ever inspected. Industry may also incur political costs, e.g., a false accusation of non-compliance. A carefully constructed compliance regime should avoid this. The Inspectorate should not be permitted to make accusations, and the inspected facility and government should be given opportunity to counter any misapprehensions.

Nonetheless, challenge inspections could carry a high political cost to the inspected facility, since it would be assumed that the inspections had legitimate reasons behind them. If they were not based on legitimate reasons, they would carry a high political cost for the BWC, as well. For this reason, it is expected that challenge inspections will be rare, and it is important that there be provisions and disincentives to prevent frivolous challenges.

As for non-challenge visits (which are now under discussion by the group), it would be interesting if a mechanism could be found to allow facilities to volunteer for them, without destroying their usefulness for validating declarations. This would remove any stigma that might be attached to an involuntary visit.

CONCLUSION

Further elaboration of these ideas and others, through collaborative efforts among government and private organizations, would likely contribute to the development of an effective compliance regime that does not impose undue burdens.

RECOGNIZING AUTHOR'S POINT OF VIEW

This activity may be used as an individualized study guide for students in libraries and resource centers or as a discussion catalyst in small group and classroom discussions.

The capacity to recognize an author's point of view is an essential reading skill. Many readers do not make clear distinctions between descriptive articles that relate factual information and articles that express a point of view. Think about the readings in Chapter Two. Are these readings essentially descriptive articles that relate factual information or articles that attempt to persuade through editorial commentary and analysis?

Guidelines

1. The following are possible descriptions of sources that appeared in Chapter Two. Choose one of the following source descriptions that best defines each source in Chapter Two.

Source Descriptions

a. Essentially an article that relates factual information.

b. Essentially an article that expresses editorial points of view.

c. Both of the above.

d. Neither of the above.

Readings in Chapter Two

_____ READING FIVE
"Biological Weapons: An Historical Perspective" by
George W. Christopher, et al.

_____ READING SIX
"The Nature of Biological Terrorism" by Col. David Franz

_____ READING SEVEN
"The Soviet Biological Warfare Program" by Richard
Preston

_____ READING EIGHT
"Aum Shinrikyo: A Germ Warfare Program" by Senate
Committee on Governmental Affairs Staff

_____ OVERVIEW
"The Biological Weapons Convention"

_____ READING NINE
"The Biological Weapons Convention: An Industrial
Perspective" by U.S. Pharmaceutical and Biotechnology
Industries

_____ READING TEN
"Making the Biological Weapons Convention Work" by
the Federation of American Scientists

2. Summarize the author's point of view in one to three sentences
for each of the readings in Chapter Two.

3. After careful consideration, pick out one reading that you think
is the most reliable source. Be prepared to explain the reasons
for your choice in a general class discussion.

CHAPTER 3

CHEMICAL AND NUCLEAR TERRORISM

THE NATURE OF CHEMICAL TERRORISM

Ron Purver

Ron Purver is a strategic analyst for the Canadian Security Intelligence Service (CSIS). The Canadian Security Intelligence Service was established in 1984, separating the activities of security intelligence from law enforcement. The organization states that its fundamental mission is to be a national intelligence organization dedicated to serving the people of Canada.

■ POINTS TO CONSIDER

1. Describe the toxicity of chemical weapons relative to other weapons.

2. What characteristics make chemical weapons attractive to terrorists?

3. Compare and contrast chemical and biological weapons.

4. Assess the feasibility of producing and deploying a chemical weapon.

Excerpted from Purver, Ron. "Chemical and Biological Terrorism: The Threat According to Open Literature." Ottawa: Canadian Security Intelligence Service, June 1995.

Despite not being as toxic as the most lethal biologi- cal agents, chemical weapons have certain other advantages that may make them more attractive to terrorists.

The toxicity of chemical agents generally falls somewhere in between that of the more deadly biological agents and that of conventional weapons, or at the lower end of the scale for weapons of mass destruction. For example, Kupperman and Trent estimate that, based on "the weight required to produce heavy casualties within a square-mile area under idealized conditions," fuel-air explosives require 320 million grams; fragmentation clus- ter bombs, 32 million; hydrocyanic acid, 32 million; mustard gas, 3.2 million; GB nerve gas, 800,000; a "crude" nuclear weapon (in terms of fissionable material only), 5,000; Type A botulinal toxin, 80; and anthrax spores, eight (Kupperman and Trent 1979: 57). Similarly, it has been estimated that it would take 100 grams of the "V" nerve agent, or almost 40 pounds of potassium cyanide, to have an effect on a water supply equivalent to just one gram of typhoid culture (SCJ 1990: 3-4). Put another way, to incapacitate or kill a person drinking less than half a cup of untreated water from a five million-liter reservoir would require no less than ten tons of potassium cyanide, compared to just 1/2 kg of *Salmonella typhi* (OTA 1991: 52).

TOXICITY

Far more toxic again are the V-agents: "VX, when inhaled, is ten times as toxic as sarin, but dermally it is 300 times as toxic" (Kupperman and Trent 1979: 65). According to Douglass and Livingstone, "the amount of VX (a nerve agent) that one can place on the head of a pin is sufficient to produce death in a human being" (1987: 17). Livingstone reports that "in tests conducted by the army, one drop of VX absorbed through the skin was enough to kill a dog" (1982: 110).

Chemical weapons such as nerve agents are generally credited with being capable of causing casualties in the range of hundreds to a few thousand (Kupperman and Trent 1979: 63 and 84; Kupperman and Woolsey 1988: 5; Mengel 1976: 446). A few authors put the total much higher, in the same range as for biolog- ical or even nuclear weapons. Thus, for example, Douglass and Livingstone write that "four tons of VX is enough to cause several hundred thousand deaths if released in aerosol form in a crowded urban area" (1987: 17). Clark goes even further, stating that "a canister of VX dropped from any tall building or sprayed over a large city from a private plane would kill millions" (1980: 110). However, most authors appear to agree with Berkowitz, et al. that "even with the best chemical agents available, if the attack effort is kept within the bounds of reason, its impact probably cannot exceed exposure of a few thousand target individuals at one time" (1972: IX-7). Berkowitz, et al. conclude: "Therefore, this is one of the lesser superviolent threats, but its small resource requirements and the great availability of necessary skills must be kept in mind" (1972: IX-7).

The final characteristics of chemical agents that should be noted here is that, in contrast to biological agents, their effects can be virtually instantaneous. In Mullen's words: "Death from organophosphate poisoning may be so rapid that the afflicted individual may be entirely unaware of what is happening" (1978: 71). According to another source, a one-milligram dose of a nerve agent "can usually kill within 15 minutes" (Joyner 1990: 137).

PUTATIVE ADVANTAGES

Despite not being as toxic as most biological agents, chemical weapons have certain other advantages that may make them more attractive to terrorists. A number of authors maintain that they are cheaper than biological agents (Douglass and Livingstone 1987: 12-13; Alexander 1983: 229; Mullins 1992: 116). For example, Livingstone cites one estimate that "the cost of producing 1,000 kg of GB (nerve agent), based on small laboratory purchases of raw materials, would be in the neighborhood of $200,000" (1986: 143). On the other hand, Douglass and Livingstone appear to contradict themselves later in citing a 1969 estimate that, "for a large-scale operation against a civilian population," casualties might cost about $600 per square kilometer with nerve-gas weapons, as compared to just one dollar with biological weapons (1987: 16). There can be no doubt, of course, that the manufacture of chemical weapons would be much less expensive than the manufacture of nuclear weapons, for terrorists or for anyone else.

It has also been said that chemical agents are "easier to use" than biological agents (Douglass and Livingstone 1987: 12). This rather vague claim could refer to a number of different aspects.

Among those noted by Douglass and Livingstone are their "stability" and the fact that they are "more containable," easily dispersed, and "controllable" ("inasmuch as they are not contagious") (1987: 12-13). Alexander agrees that "their delivery systems are manageable, and their dispersal techniques are efficient" (1983: 229); Mullins that "dispersal is easy and widespread," as well as being "fairly easy to control" (1992: 116). On this latter point Mullins elaborates: "The use of chemical agents could be controlled to a much greater extent than could nuclear or biological agents. The delivery of chemical agents could be accomplished with exact precision, thus insuring that only the target audience was affected" (1992: 111, 116). On the other hand, Mengel argues that, by comparison to biological agents, "chemical technologies...are practically limited by delivery problems" (1976: 446).

EASE OF MANUFACTURE

Douglass and Livingstone have also referred to the relative "ease of manufacture" of chemical, as compared to biological, agents (1987: 13). At the same time, however, in another apparent contradiction, they argue that "whereas chemical weapons require a 'moderately advanced chemical technique,' the raw materials for a biological weapon are readily accessible in most countries and should present little difficulty to terrorists" (1987: 23). Alexander simply describes chemical weapons as "relatively easy to obtain" (1983: 229), thus leaving open the question of manufacture or acquisition by other means. As to the latter point, Yevgeny Primakov, the head of the Russian Foreign Intelligence Service, has noted that "an additional temptation for the employment of chemical weapons for terrorist purposes is the rather wide employment of toxic substances by the police and special purpose forces of a number of countries" (1993: 5). It is unclear here, however, whether Primakov is referring to the opportunities thereby created for the theft of such material, or rather to the precedent of its being used. Regarding the first of these alternatives, Mullins suggests that, due to the putatively lower level of security surrounding chemical weapons storage sites as compared to nuclear or biological facilities, chemical agents would be the easiest to steal (1992: 109).

In their assessment of the comparative advantages of chemical and biological agents for terrorist use, Kupperman and Trent note that "there is limited commercial availability of deadly pathogens. Moreover, the growth, care, and dispersion of biological agents

76

require more technological sophistication than does the dispensing of chemicals" (1979: 85). Similarly, Mengel refers to chemical agents as "requiring the least amount of resources to manufacture of the technologies examined" (1976: 446). On the other hand, Hurwitz avers, without further elaboration, that "it may be even easier for terrorists to acquire biological weapons than it would be for them to acquire chemical weapons" (1982: 38). Mullins appears to agree with this assessment by locating chemical terrorism "on the continuum midway between the technology required to manufacture a nuclear device, and the ease of using biological agents" (1992: 108).

Unlike the case with biological agents, there appears to be a widespread consensus on the level of skill required for the production of a chemical agent: namely, that of a graduate student in chemistry (Clark 1980: 110; Jenkins and Rubin 1978: 223; Mullen 1978: 72; Hurwitz 1982: 38). In this regard, many authors refer to the need for nothing more than a "moderately competent chemist" (Kupperman and Trent 1979: 64; Barnaby 1992: 85-6), or even "any competent scientist" (Clark 1980: 110). There does, however, appear to be some difference of opinion over whether a single individual is likely to be capable of both producing a chemical weapon and employing it effectively in a terrorist attack.

LIKELY TYPES OF AGENTS

As in the case of biological agents, a large number of chemical substances have been identified as being of potential interest to terrorists. According to Kupperman and Kamen, "there are literally tens of thousands of highly poisonous chemicals" (1989: 101). Mullen cites an estimate of "well over 50,000" for the number of different organophosphate compounds alone (1978: 69). Those agents specifically mentioned in the literature on CB terrorism include: insecticides such as nicotine sulfate, DFP (diisopropyl-phosphorofluoridate), parathion, and TEPP; herbicides such as 2, 4D and 2,4,5T (against plants), TCDD (dioxin), and benzidine (112-14); "blood agents" such as hydrogen cyanide and cyanogen chloride; "choking agents" such as chlorine, phosgene (carbonyl chloride), and chloropicrin; "blistering agents" such as sulfur mustard, nitrogen mustard, and lewisite; and "nerve agents" such as tabun, sarin, VX, and soman. Other chemicals mentioned include: Prussic acid (hydrocyanic acid), lysergic acid diethylamide (LSD), aminazin, pheromones, pure nicotine, phosgene oxime (CX), arsenic, Cobalt-60, compound 1080, arsine, nickel carbonyl, sodium fluoroacetate, and strychnine.

MEANS OF ACQUISITION

According to Kupperman and Trent, "For small, not widely destructive terrorist acts, household cleaning agents could prove lethal. Certainly, the more toxic insecticides, such as parathion or TEPP, although requiring an exterminator's license, are essentially unregulated items" (1979: 84). The latter two agents, by another account, are "almost as toxic as their military counterparts" (Kupperman and Woolsey 1988: 4). Berkowitz, et al. highlight the danger of theft of such materials, noting that "truckload quantities of parathion are on the highways daily" and that "a hijacked truckload certainly poses a potential threat" (Berkowitz, et al. 1972: VIII-32).

MEANS OF DELIVERY

As in the case of biological agents, most authors consider the effective delivery of chemical agents to their target as being more difficult than their manufacture. Most authors agree that the most feasible "mass" chemical attack would be one limited to the enclosed spaces of a single, discrete facility such as a hotel, office building, or convention center (Jenkins and Rubin 1978: 224), with a resulting casualty toll ranging between a few hundred and several thousand.

Other possible means of delivering chemical agents to their targets, though on a smaller scale, would be through the contamination of foodstuffs or by direct contact. Livingstone, for example, suggests that "it would be possible to inject a chemical poison into a victim by means of a hypodermic needle concealed in the tip of an umbrella" (1982: 111). Mullins adds that "chemical agents could be used effectively as contaminants for projectiles such as bullets, flechettes, and shrapnel" (1992: 111).

BIBLIOGRAPHY

Alexander, Yonah. "Terrorism and High-Technology Weapons." **Perspectives on Terrorism.** ed. Lawrence Z. Freedman and Yonah Alexander. Wilmington, DE: Scholarly Resources, Inc., 1983.

Barnaby, Frank. **The Role and Control of Weapons in the 1990s.** London: Routledge, 1992.

Berkowitz, B.J., et al. **Superviolence: The Civil Threat of Mass Destruction Weapons.** Santa Barbara, CA: ADCON (Advanced Concepts Research) Corporation, Report A72-034-10, September 29, 1972.

Clark, Richard Charles. **Technological Terrorism.** Old Greenwich, CT: Devin-Adair, 1980.

Douglass, Joseph D., Jr., and Neil C. Livingstone. **America the Vulnerable: The Threat of Chemical and Biological Warfare.** Lexington, MA: Lexington Books, 1987.

Hurwitz, Elliott. "Terrorists and Chemical/Biological Weapons." **Naval War College Review,** 35:3. May-June 1982: 36-40.

Jenkins, Brian M., and Alfred P. Rubin. "New Vulnerabilities and the Acquisition of New Weapons by Nongovernment Groups." **Legal Aspects of International Terrorism.** ed. Alona E. Evans and John F. Murphy. Lexington, MA: Lexington Books, 1978.

Joyner, Christopher C. "Chemoterrorism: Rethinking the Reality of the Threat." **The 1988-89 Annual on Terrorism.** ed. Yonah Alexander and H. Foxman. The Netherlands: Kluwer Academic Publishers, 1990.

Kupperman, Robert H., and Jeff Kamen. **Final Warning: Averting Disaster in the New Age of Terrorism.** New York: Doubleday, 1989.

Kupperman, Robert H., and Darrell M. Trent. **Terrorism: Threat, Reality, Response.** Stanford, CA: Hoover Institution Press, 1979.

Kupperman, Robert H., and R. James Woolsey. Testimony before the Technology and Law Subcommittee of the Judiciary Committee. May 19, 1988.

Livingstone, Neil C. "The Impact of Technological Innovation." **Hydra of Carnage.** ed. Uri Ra'anan, et al. Lexington, MA: Lexington Books, 1986.

Livingstone, Neil C. **The War Against Terrorism.** Toronto: Lexington Books, 1982.

Mengel, R.W. "Terrorism and New Technologies of Destruction: An Overview of the Potential Risk." **Disorders and Terrorism: Report of the Task Force on Disorders and Terrorism.** Washington, D.C.: National Advisory Committee on Criminal Justice Standards & Goals, 1976.

Mullen, Robert K. Mass Destruction and Terrorism. **Journal of International Affairs,** 32:1. Spring-Summer 1978: 62-89.

Mullins, Wayman C. "An Overview and Analysis of Nuclear, Biological, and Chemical Terrorism: The Weapons, Strategies and Solutions to a Growing Problem." **American Journal of Criminal Justice,** 16:2. 1992: 95-119.

Primakov, Yevgeny. **A New Challenge after the "Cold War": The Proliferation of Weapons of Mass Destruction.** Moscow: Foreign Intelligence Service of the Russian Federation, 1993.

THE IRAQI USE OF CHEMICAL WAR: TEN YEARS AFTER HALABJA

Christine M. Gosden, M.D.

Christine M. Gosden traveled to Iraq on a humanitarian mission to treat and study the victims of the chemical weapons attack in Halabja. She is a professor of Medical Genetics at the University of Liverpool. Formerly, Gosden worked for the British Medical Research Council.

■ POINTS TO CONSIDER

1. Explain the significance of the city of Halabja.

2. Summarize the events that led to the attack in 1988.

3. What separates the incident from other attacks of the same nature?

4. Describe the long-term problems of Halabja.

Excerpted from the testimony of Christine Gosden before the Subcommittee on Technology, Terrorism and Government of the U.S. Senate Judiciary Committee and the U.S. Senate Select Committee on Intelligence, April 22, 1998.

I know I must do everything I can to help the people of Halabja affected by the winds of death and destruction wrought by clouds of toxic weapons.

Chemical and biological weapons are not humane weapons which kill rapidly and mercifully. I have recently witnessed the long-term effects of the chemical weapons attack on the large civilian population in Northern Iraq, in the town of Halabja. I was shocked by the devastating effects of these weapons which have caused problems such as cancers, blindness and congenital mal-formations. My experiences of the devastating power of these weapons have emphasized the importance of protecting individu-als and nations against chemical and biological weapons attacks. Having seen and experienced their suffering and heard their pleas for help, I know I must do everything I can to help the people of Halabja and enter into a partnership with them to try to find effec-tive therapies for bodies, minds and spirits which have been affected by the winds of death and destruction wrought by clouds of toxic weapons.

THE ATTACK ON HALABJA

Let me begin by describing the poison gas attack on the Iraqi town of Halabja. This was the largest-scale chemical weapons (CW) attack against a civilian population in modern times.

Halabja was a bustling city in Northern Iraq with a population which was predominantly Kurdish and had sympathized with Iran during the Iran-Iraq war in the 1980s. The population at the time of the attack was about 80,000 people. Troops from the Kurdish Patriotic Union of Kurdistan (PUK) entered Halabja on March 15, 1988, amidst heavy resistance from Iraqi security and military forces.

Halabja fell to the PUK troops (accompanied by Iranian revolu-tionary guards) four hours later. The Iraqis responded with heavy artillery fire and an early wave of six aircraft bombarded an area near Halabja with ordinary high explosives. The civilians had been prevented from leaving the town by the PUK, hoping that the Iraqis would not attack a town with civilians in it – thus providing a human shield.

The CW attack began early in the evening of March 16, when a group of eight aircraft began dropping chemical bombs; the chemical bombardment continued all night. According to Kurdish commanders on the scene, there were 14 aircraft sorties during the night, with seven to eight planes in each group, and they concentrated their attack on the city and all the roads leading out of Halabja. The chemical attacks continued until the 19th.

Let me emphasize that this was not the first chemical attack by Saddam Hussein. Previous attacks had been launched by Iraqi aircraft against 20 small villages in 1987. However, the scale and intensity of the chemical campaign against Halabja was entirely different – this was the first time that chemical weapons had been used on a major civilian population of this size. The victims of the attack included women, children and the elderly.

CHEMICAL "COCKTAIL"

There is something else that sets Halabja apart from other known chemical weapons attacks. The Halabja attack involved multiple chemical agents – including mustard gas, and the nerve agents sarin, tabun and VX. Some sources report that cyanide was also used. It may be that an impure form of tabun, which has a cyanide residue, released the cyanide compound. Most attempts directed to developing strategies against chemical or biological weapons have been directed towards a single threat. The attack on Halabja illustrates the importance of careful tactical planning directed towards more than one agent, and specific knowledge about the effects of each of the agents.

Exposed civilians are particularly at risk if a war strategy aims to produce civilian casualties on a large scale. Developing medical treatment regimes for trained military personnel, who are generally young, healthy and of approximately the same weight and size, is challenging enough. But the demands of developing effective treatment regimes for children, the elderly and infirm is even more daunting. And the task is even more daunting when having to treat a chemical weapons "cocktail."

Saddam Hussein clearly intended to complicate the task of treating the Halabja victims. At a minimum, he was using Halabja as part of the Iraqi CW test program. Handbooks for doctors in Iraqi military show sophisticated medical knowledge of the effects of CW. The Iraqi military used mustard gas in the "cocktail," for which there is no defense or antidote. And it is also worth noting that Saddam did not use the nerve agent soman, but instead used

Cartoon by Joe Heller.

tabun, sarin and VX, as I said above. This is noteworthy because it shows that Hussein's experts were also well aware that pyridostigmine bromide – one of the chief treatments against nerve agent – is relatively ineffective against tabun, sarin and VX, but highly effective against soman, the only agent he did not use.

LONG TERM EFFECTS

It is important to remember the basic tenets of humanitarian efforts and the internationally recognized purposes of medicine and medical research which are to maintain health, relieve human suffering and prevent death from disease. In the case of Halabja, all of these seem to have been overlooked or forgotten and we have so far failed to understand what has happened to these people or helped them effectively.

There had been no systematic and detailed research study carried out in Halabja in the ten years since the attack. The novel effects such as those on reproductive function, congenital malformations, long term neurological and neuropsychiatric effects, (especially on those who were very young at the time) and cancers in women and children are of special importance. There is no knowledge about the ways in which the serious and long term damage caused by these weapons can be treated. For example, the eye, respiratory and neuropsychiatric problems do not appear to respond to conventional therapy.

And so, I set about to determine the long-term effects of chemical weapons attack, using the Halabja attack as a case study. It has been a collaborative research project with the doctors and people of Halabja and Souleymania. What we have found is sobering, if not frightening. It must serve as a wake-up call to all of us about the need for improving our medical preparedness and national and international response plans to chemical weapons attack.

The list of the serious long term effects of these weapons is in itself evidence of the terrible effects of these weapons:

1. Respiratory problems
2. Eye problems
3. Skin problems
4. Neuropsychiatric problems
5. Cancers – head, neck, respiratory tract, skin, gastrointestinal tract, leukemias and lymphomas (especially in children), and reproductive (including breast and ovary)
6. Congenital abnormalities
7. Infertility
8. Miscarriages, stillbirths, neonatal and infant deaths.

Many of the people in Halabja have two or more major problems. Thus someone may be blind as a result of the attack, still have serious skin burns and have respiratory problems. Their difficulties may continue, too, because of the increased risks of cancers of all types including leukemias and lymphomas, which are very common. The occurrences of genetic mutations and carcinogenesis in this population appear comparable with those who were one to two kilometers from ground zero in Hiroshima and Nagasaki, and show that the chemicals used in the attack have a general effect on the body similar to that of ionizing radiation.

Many people have expressed their astonishment that since the people were bombarded with this awful cocktail of weapons, they do not all have identical problems. I think there are several reasons for this. Some people received different doses; some were drenched in liquid mustard gas and nerve agents, others breathed in vapor; some people were outside, others were inside; and some were wrapped in clothing or wet sheets or washed off the chemicals quickly. It's also important to note that people vary in their ability to detoxify and this is genetically determined. Finally, the

DNA target for the mutagenesis is the whole of the human genome. Many different genes may be affected in the body, conferring risks of cancer or disease, and in eggs or sperm, causing congenital abnormalities or lethality in offspring.

A great deal remains unknown. The long-term effects such as those on fertility and congenital malformations are not well characterized. The most effective ways of treating the long-term problems are not known. For example, should there be attempts to treat the blindness resulting from the corneal blistering and scarring with corneal transplants or would the pain be best treated with medicated contact lenses or special artificial tears? It is important, too, for research and therapy to be undertaken in a concerted and thoughtful way with the patients being fully involved in the research and as partners in devising effective methods for treatment.

MEDICAL PREPAREDNESS

In order to provide effective defense against chemical and biological weapons attacks, there is a need for a good comprehensive working knowledge of the chemical and biological weapons which all the major military powers have stockpiled. This has to be coupled with an understanding of the principal ways of deploying each of the different types of weapons and the likely civilian and military targets against which they might be deployed. The principal methods of defense against each of these weapons, such as decontamination methods, antidotes and methods of treating casualties to prevent long-term effects are extremely important.

Political skill and diplomacy to prevent the use of these weapons, either in terrorist attacks, civil wars or in major or minor conflicts must be the major target. It is obvious from studies of the effects of these weapons that there are virtually no humane chemical or biological weapons. These weapons can kill, maim and produce life-long damage on the populations they are used against and, if mutagenic and carcinogenic chemicals are deployed, can damage future generations, long after the immediate effects of the attack have appeared to recede. We owe future generations a heritage free from threat, pain, disfigurement and handicap.

CHEMICAL WEAPONS, THEIR EFFECTS, AND TREATMENT FOR EXPOSURE TO THEM.

Table 1.

Agent	Toxicity	Signs and Symptoms	Antidote	Care
Blister agents Nitrogen mustard Sulfur mustard	Delayed effects; large dose life-threatening if untreated.	Erythema, burns, vesication; eye lung and skin damage; respiratory and hematological effects; sepsis.	None; decontamination within 2 min. to prevent tissue damage.	Burn care, eye therapy, pulmonary support.
Nerve agents GA (tabun) GB (sarin) GD (soman) VX	Immediately life-threatening	Eye, nose, lung and GI effects. Large dose; loss of consciousness, convulsions, cessation of respiration, flaccid paralysis.	Atropine sulfate, pralidoxime (Protopam) chloride.	Administration of antidotes, ventilation, administration of diazepam (Valium).
Cyanide Hydrocyanic acid Cyanogen chloride	Immediately life-threatening	Inhalation: convulsions, death Ingestion: dizziness, nausea, vomiting, weakness, respiratory distress, loss of consciousness, convulsions, apnea, death.	Amyl nitrite, sodium nitrite, sodium thiosulfate.	Administration of antidotes, supplemental oxygen.

*Adapted from Army FMB-285, Navy NAVMED P-5041, Air Force AFM 160-11 Field Manual. The Treatment of Chemical Agent Casualties and Conventional Military Chemical Injuries, Washington, D.C.: The Departments of the Army, The Navy, and the Air Force, February 28, 1990.

THE CHEMICAL WEAPONS CONVENTION: AN OVERVIEW

More than 100 years of international efforts to ban chemical weapons culminated January 13, 1993, in the signing of the Chemical Weapons Convention (CWC). The Convention entered into force April 29, 1997. One hundred twelve of the 168 signatories have ratified the Convention as of July 20, 1998.

On April 24, 1998, the U.S. Senate passed the CWC resolution of ratification (S.Res. 75) by a vote of 74-26. President Clinton signed the resolution and the United States became the 75th nation to ratify the Convention. Russia and Iran were the most recent nations to have ratified the CWC.

The CWC bans the development, production, stockpiling, and use of chemical weapons by member signatories. It also requires the destruction of all chemical weapons stockpiles and production facilities. The Convention provides the most extensive and intrusive verification regime of any arms control treaty, extending its coverage to not only governmental but also civilian facilities. The Convention also requires export controls and reporting requirements on chemicals that can be used as warfare agents and their precursors. The CWC establishes the Organization for the Prohibition of Chemical Weapons (OPCW) to oversee the Convention's implementation.

Excerpted from Bowman, Steven R., "Chemical Weapons Convention: Issues for Congress, (updated)," **CRS Issue Brief.** Washington, D.C.: Congressional Research Service, August 3, 1998.

Chemical Weapons Convention implementing legislation, as S. 610, passed the Senate unanimously on May 23, 1997. This legislation, which was an amendment in the nature of a substitute reported from the Judiciary Committee, provides the statutory authority for domestic compliance with the Convention's provisions. It sets criminal and civil penalties for the development, production, acquisition, stockpiling, transfer, possession, or use of chemical weapons. It also establishes: 1) procedures for seizure, forfeiture, and destruction of contraband chemical weapons; 2) statutory authority for record keeping and reporting requirements relevant to the CWC; 3) various restrictions on certain chemicals, depending on their likelihood of being used to produce chemical weapons; and 4) a protective regime for confidential business information gathered from private corporations. S. 610 also provides detailed procedures to be used for on-site inspections by the OPCW, including limitations on access and search warrant procedures, should they be required.

Though supporting passage, CWC advocates expressed concerns over several sections of the legislation which were added in Judiciary Committee mark-up, and intended to work for their revision before final enactment. However, S. 610 was incorporated without amendment as Title II of Iran missile sanctions legislation (H.R. 2709), which, because of objections to the missile sanctions element of the legislation, was vetoed by the President, leaving the future of implementing legislation uncertain.

Without the legal authority to collect the needed data, the United States is delinquent in its initial declarations to the OPCW and hence in technical violation of the Convention, as are several other nations also experiencing bureaucratic or legislative delays.

READING

13

THE CHEMICAL WEAPONS CONVENTION JEOPARDIZES SECURITY

Malcolm Forbes, Jr.

*Malcolm Forbes, Jr., is the President and CEO of Forbes, Inc.,
New York. In the following reading, Forbes advises against
congressional ratification of the Chemical Weapons Convention
(CWC).*

■ **POINTS TO CONSIDER**

1. Why does Forbes equate the CWC with an unfunded mandate?

2. Describe the ways which the CWC compromises national security,
   according to the author.

3. Explain the constitutional concerns highlighted in the reading.

4. Discuss the issue of barriers to entry. How does the CWC,
   in the author's estimation, stand to hurt small businesses
   disproportionately?

Excerpted from the testimony of Malcolm Forbes, Jr., before the U.S. Senate Committee
on Foreign Relations, April 15, 1997.

Historically, phony arms control treaties have invariably translated into reduced efforts by the democracies to defend themselves against the predatory dictatorships.

There are many compelling reasons to oppose ratification of the Chemical Weapons Convention (CWC). The fact is that the Chemical Weapons Convention significantly threatens the freedoms we Americans cherish, significantly diminishes America's sovereignty, and, significantly increases America's vulnerability to chemical warfare. It is as though we were being asked to endorse a drug that worsens the disease it purports to cure and, in addition, has some highly dangerous side effects.

LOSING THE COMPETITIVE ADVANTAGE

To explain just how dangerous the CWC's side effects are, let me ask a simple question: What is the basis of America's greatness? Why is it that although the international arena contains many powers, we are the world's sole superpower? Any adequate answer to this question would have to include such factors as the competitive nature of our free market system, the unparalleled technological sophistication of American enterprises, and, most important, our basic freedom. These are the sinews of our power, the basis of our national greatness. Yet it is precisely these quintessentially American strengths that the Convention would undermine.

Let me begin by talking about American competitiveness. As I have strenuously argued on other occasions, maintaining America's competitive edge requires a lessening of the tax and regulatory burdens on the American people and our Nation's enterprises. Unfortunately, the CWC will have precisely the opposite effect. It will burden up to 8,000 companies across the United States with major new reporting, regulatory and inspection requirements entailing large and uncompensated compliance costs. These added costs constitute an added federal mandate. Like so many unfunded mandates, they are bound to retard our economic growth and make our companies less competitive.

PIRATING SECRETS

But it gets worse. For in addition to the costs arising from heavy-duty reporting, the Chemical Weapons Convention subjects our chemical companies to snap inspections that will allow other nations access to our latest chemical equipment and information. No longer will violators of intellectual property rights in China, Iran and elsewhere have to go to the trouble of pirating our secrets; incredibly, we ourselves will hand them the stuff on a silver platter. It is no that wonder that former CIA Director and Secretary of Defense James Schlesinger has called the Convention a "godsend" for foreign intelligence services.

IN CONFLICT WITH THE CONSTITUTION

But it gets worse. The CWC threatens the constitutional rights guaranteed Americans under the Fourth Amendment. As former Defense Secretaries Dick Cheney, Donald Rumsfeld and Caspar Weinberger noted in a joint letter to Majority Leader Trent Lott, "the CWC will jeopardize U.S. citizens' constitutional rights by requiring the U.S. government to permit searches without either warrants or probable cause."

"Jeopardize U.S. citizens' constitutional rights" – think about that. And think about all the criminal cases that our courts have summarily dismissed because, in their view, the defendants' constitutional rights had been violated by police searches conducted without "probable cause." Are America's businesses to receive less justice than suspected felons? Of course not – the very idea is preposterous! And yet, that is precisely what compliance with the CWC would entail.

But it gets worse. In addition to threatening our Fourth Amendment rights, the Convention also undercuts our Fifth Amendment rights against having our property taken by the government without just compensation. As Judge Robert Bork noted in a letter to Sen. Orrin Hatch:

> "Fifth Amendment problems arise from the authority of inspectors to collect data and analyze samples. This may constitute an illegal seizure and, perhaps, constitute the taking of private property by the government without compensation. The foreign inspectors will not be subject to punishment for any theft of proprietary information."

BARRIERS TO ENTRY

There is yet another pernicious aspect of this Convention that I would like to touch on – the very different impact it would have on large and small companies. As former Secretary of Defense Donald Rumsfeld noted in testimony before this Committee, big companies are generally better able than small companies to withstand additional reporting, regulatory and/or government inspection requirements. Some might even regard such burdens as a barrier to entry that can enhance their market-share at the expense of their smaller competitors.

Large chemical manufacturers are among the most pervasively regulated industries in the world. These companies can reasonably conclude that the burdens of this Convention are manageable.

The same certainly cannot be said of smaller, less regulated companies – many of whom still seem to be unaware that this treaty could adversely affect them and their bottom lines. The array of American companies that fall into this category is simply mindboggling. They include those in such diverse fields as electronics, plastics, automotive, biotech, food processing, brewers, distillers, textiles, non-nuclear electric utility operators, detergents and soaps, cosmetics and fragrances, paints, and even manufacturers of ballpoint pen ink. The Senate would be ill-advised to ratify a Convention that could harm so many American enterprises without having truly compelling reasons to do so.

UNDERCUTTING NATIONAL SECURITY

Finally, in discussing the harmful side effects of the Chemical Weapons Convention, I would like to draw attention to Articles X and XI. These provisions, which obligate the signatories to "facilitate the fullest possible exchange" of technology directly relevant to chemical war-fighting, will be cited by other governments – and, probably, by some American companies – as pretexts for doing business with Iran and Cuba, with adverse consequences for U.S. national security interests.

These, then, are some of the costs associated with ratification of the Chemical Weapons Convention. They are unacceptably high. Are there any offsetting benefits? Unfortunately, the answer is no, there are not. In fact, far from protecting us against an outbreak of chemical warfare, the Convention would increase the likelihood of these awful weapons being used. As former Defense Secretaries James Schlesinger, Caspar Weinberger and Donald Rumsfeld wrote in the *Washington Post* (March 5, 1997), "The CWC would likely have the effect of leaving the United States and its allies more, not less, vulnerable to chemical attack."

FALSE SECURITY

How would the CWC increase our vulnerability to chemical attack? By giving rise to a false sense of security and a diminished program for defending our troops and people against the danger of chemical attack. By leading the American people to believe that with this Convention we have somehow rid the world of chemical weapons when, in fact, even the CWC's defenders acknowledge that it will be unverifiable, unenforceable and ineffective in globally banning chemical weapons. Historically, phony arms control treaties have invariably translated into reduced efforts by the democracies to defend themselves against the predatory dictatorships. Sadly, there is no reason to suppose that the Chemical Weapons Convention will prove an exception to this general rule.

THE CHEMICAL WEAPONS CONVENTION NEEDS RATIFICATION

Madeleine K. Albright

Madeleine Korbel Albright was sworn in as 64th U.S. Secretary of State on January 23, 1997. She is the highest ranking woman in the U.S. government. Prior to her appointment, Albright served as the U.S. Permanent Representative to the United Nations and as a member of President Clinton's Cabinet and National Security Council. In addition, Albright has extensive experience in public policy research and academia and has written and taught concerning Central and Eastern European and Russian affairs.

■ POINTS TO CONSIDER

1. What type of influence does Albright believe the U.S. has on the world community?

2. Explain the importance of U.S. signatory status to the Chemical Weapons Convention.

3. Discuss the justification for the U.S. to give up chemical weapons.

4. Evaluate Albright's answers to the critics of U.S. congressional ratification of the Chemical Weapons Convention. (Also see the previous reading for criticisms of CWC.)

Excerpted from the testimony of Madeleine K. Albright before the U.S. Senate Committee on Foreign Relations, April 8, 1997.

Chemical weapons are inhumane. They kill horribly, massively, and – once deployed – are no more controllable than the wind.

The United States is the only nation with the power, influence, and respect to forge a strong global consensus against the spread of weapons of mass destruction. In recent years, we have used our position wisely to gain the removal of nuclear weapons from Ukraine, Belarus, and Kazakhstan. We have led in securing the extension of the Nuclear Nonproliferation Treaty. We have frozen North Korea's nuclear program. We have maintained sanctions against Iraq. And we have joined forces with more than two dozen other major countries in controlling the transfer of dangerous conventional arms and sensitive dual-use goods and technologies.

THE HORROR OF CHEMICAL WEAPONS

Chemical weapons are inhumane. They kill horribly, massively, and – once deployed – are no more controllable than the wind. That is why the United States decided – under a law signed by President Reagan in 1985 – to destroy the vast majority of our chemical weapons stockpiles by the year 2004.

We must bear in mind that today, keeping and producing chemical weapons are legal. The gas Saddam Hussein used to massacre Kurdish villagers in 1988 was produced legally. In most countries, terrorists can produce or procure chemical agents, such as sarin gas, legally. Regimes such as Iran and Libya can build up their stockpiles of chemical weapons legally.

If we are ever to rid the world of these horrible weapons, we must begin by making not only their use, but also their development, production, acquisition, and stockpiling illegal. This is fundamental. This is especially important now when America's comparative military might is so great that an attack by unconventional means may hold for some potential adversaries their only perceived hope of success. And making chemical weapons illegal is the purpose of the Chemical Weapons Convention (CWC).

THE NEED FOR THE CONVENTION

The CWC sets the standard that it is wrong for any nation to build or possess a chemical weapon, and gives us strong and effective tools for enforcing that standard. This is not a magic wand. It will not eliminate all danger. It will not allow us to relax or cease to ensure the full preparedness of our armed forces against the threat of chemical weapons. What it will do is make chemical weapons harder for terrorists or outlaw states to buy, build or conceal.

Under the treaty, parties will be required to give up the chemical weapons they have, and to refrain from developing, producing or acquiring such weapons in the future. To enforce these requirements, the most comprehensive and intense inspection regime ever negotiated will be put in place. Parties will also be obliged to enact and enforce laws to punish violators within their jurisdictions.

Of course, no treaty is 100 percent verifiable, but this treaty provides us valuable tools for monitoring chemical weapons proliferation worldwide – a task we will have to do with or without the CWC.

PUNISHING VIOLATORS

CWC inspections and monitoring will help us learn more about chemical weapons programs. It will also enable us to act on the information we obtain. In the future, countries known to possess chemical weapons, who have joined the CWC, will be forced to choose between compliance and sanctions. And countries outside the CWC will be subject to trade restrictions whether or not they are known to possess chemical arms.

These penalties would not exist without the treaty. They will make it more costly for any nation to have chemical weapons, and more difficult for rogue states or terrorists to acquire materials needed to produce them.

SETTING AN EXAMPLE

Over time, I believe that – if the United States joins the CWC – most other countries will, too. Consider that there are now 185 members of the Nuclear Nonproliferation Treaty, and only five outside. Most nations play by the rules and want the respect and benefits the world bestows upon those who do.

But the problem states will never accept a prohibition on chemical weapons if America stays out, keeps them company and gives them cover. We will not have the standing to mobilize our allies to support strong action against violators if we ourselves have refused to join the treaty being violated.

The core question here is who do we want to set the standards? Critics suggest that the CWC is flawed because we cannot assume early ratification and full compliance by the outlaw states. To me, that is like saying that because some people smuggle drugs, we should enact no law against drug smuggling. When it comes to the protection of Americans, the lowest common denominator is not good enough. Those who abide by the law, not those who break it, must establish the rules by which all should be judged.

BIPARTISAN AND MILITARY SUPPORT

Eliminating chemical weapons has long been a bipartisan goal. The Convention itself is the product of years of effort by leaders from both parties.

Just recently, we received a letter of support signed by 17 former four star generals and admirals, including three of the former chairmen of the Joint Chiefs of Staff and five former service chiefs. In their words:

> "Each of us can point to decades of military experience in command positions. We have all trained and commanded troops to prepare for the wartime use of chemical weapons and for defenses against them. Our focus is not on the treaty's limitations, but instead on its many strengths. The CWC destroys stockpiles that could threaten our troops; it significantly improves our intelligence capabilities; and it creates new international sanctions to punish those states who remain outside of the treaty. For these reasons, we strongly support the CWC."

ANSWERING CRITICS

Critics have asserted that the CWC obliges member states to exchange manufacturing technology that can be used to make chemical agents. This is untrue. The CWC prohibits members from providing any assistance that would contribute to chemical weapons proliferation.

Nothing in the CWC requires any weakening of our export controls. Further, the United States will continue to work through

RIOT CONTROL AGENTS (RCAs)

The Convention permits RCA use for "law enforcement including domestic riot control purposes." However, it prohibits the use of riot control agents as a "method of warfare."

This interpretation allows the use of RCA in riot control situations in areas under direct and distinct U.S. military control, to include controlling rioting prisoners of war and in rear echelon areas outside the zone of immediate combat to protect convoys from civil disturbance, terrorist and paramilitary organizations. However, it prohibits the use of RCA solely against combatants, and, according to the current international understanding, even for humanitarian purposes in situations where combatants and noncombatants are intermingled.

Excerpted from the testimony of former U.S. Chairman, Joint Chiefs of Staff, John Shalikashvili before the U.S. Senate Committee on Armed Services, August 11, 1994.

the Australia Group to maintain and make more effective internationally agreed controls on chemical and biological weapons technology. And, as I have said, the CWC establishes tough restrictions on the transfer of precursor chemicals and other materials that might help a nation or terrorist group to acquire chemical weapons.

Opponents also suggest that if we ratify the CWC, we will become complacent about the threat that chemical weapons pose. This, too, is false – and this body can help ensure it remains false. The President has requested an increase of almost $225 million over five years in our already robust program to equip and train our troops against chemical and biological attack. We are also proceeding with theater missile defense programs and intelligence efforts against the chemical threat.

Some critics of the treaty have expressed the fear that its inspection requirements could raise constitutional problems here in the United States. However, the CWC provides explicitly that inspections will be conducted according to each nation's constitutional processes.

Another issue that arose early in the debate was that the CWC could become a regulatory nightmare for small businesses here in the United States. But after reviewing the facts, the National Federation of Independent Business concluded that its members "will not be affected" by the treaty.

CONCLUSION

By ratifying the CWC, we will assume the lead in shaping a new and effective legal regime. We will be in a position to challenge those who refuse to give up these poisonous weapons. We will provide an added measure of security for the men and women of our armed forces. We will protect American industry and American jobs. And we will make our citizens safer than they would be in a world where chemical arms remain legal.

This treaty is about other people's weapons, not our own. It reflects existing American practices and advances enduring American interests. It is right and smart for America.

15

THE PLAGUE OF NUCLEAR TERRORISM

Jessica Eve Stern

Jessia Eve Stern is the former director for Russian and Ukranian Affairs at the National Security Council.

■ POINTS TO CONSIDER

1. Describe the security conditions in the former Soviet Union for many nuclear facilities.

2. According to Stern, how have terrorists changed their tactics? Explain nuclear weapons' place with regard to the new terrorist tactics.

3. Discuss the author's policy proposals to maintain the facilities and human capital of the former Soviet Union.

Excerpted from the testimony of Jessica Eve Stern before the Subcommittee on Military Research and Development of the U.S. House of Representatives Committee on National Security, October 7, 1997.

Hundreds of tons of plutonium and highly enriched uranium – the essential ingredient of nuclear weapons – are spread at some forty sites throughout the former Soviet Union. Some of this material is secured with the equivalent of bicycle locks.

Director of Central Intelligence George Tenet has warned that "fanatical" terrorists pose an "unprecedented threat" to the United States. Tenet also testified that the CIA is increasingly seeing terrorist groups looking into the feasibility and effectiveness of chemical, biological, and nuclear weapons. His predecessor, John Deutch, testified that nuclear materials and technologies are "more accessible now than at any other time in history." And yet, to date, U.S. budgetary priorities do not reflect these assessments. Only a tiny fraction of our defense dollars directly address these threats.

CLIMATE OF FEAR

Americans are increasingly fearful of terrorism involving weapons of mass destruction, according to a recent poll. There is no question that Americans are right to be afraid. Crude designs for nuclear, chemical, and biological weapons are increasingly available in book form and on the Internet. Nuclear and chemical weapons components are leaking from poorly guarded facilities in the former Soviet Union. Closer to home, extremists and cults are experimenting with weapons of mass destruction. In the last several years, right-wing extremists have planned to use ricin, an extremely toxic biological agent, and in a separate incident, nuclear materials, to kill IRS and other U.S. government officials. Cults are expected to become even more violent in the next few years: the final years of a century have often been met with acts of extreme violence, and the end of the millennium may provoke even more extreme outbursts.

Nuclear, chemical, and biological weapons may be uniquely attractive to terrorists seeking to conjure a sense of divine retribution, to display scientific prowess, to kill large numbers, to invoke a deep sense of dread, or to retaliate against states that have used these weapons in the past. Research on risk perception shows that poisons – including radioactive materials – have many characteristics common to risks that are disproportionately feared, including invisibility, delayed effects, the potential for catastrophe, and

102

the victim's inability to control exposure. Fear of these weapons enhances their military effectiveness, and even more so, their effectiveness as terror weapons.

LOOSE NUKES AND POISONS

Hundreds of tons of plutonium and highly enriched uranium – the essential ingredient of nuclear weapons – are spread at some forty sites throughout the former Soviet Union. Some of this material is secured with the equivalent of bicycle locks. Of particular concern is a reactor at Aktau, Kazakhstan, where three tons of "ivory grade" plutonium are stored directly across the Caspian Sea from Iran.

Even more troubling is the prospect that terrorists could acquire bombs ready-made. Senior Russian officials have expressed grave concerns about inadequate security for warheads in transit as well as in storage. The Russian military reportedly claims that it faces "chronic shortages" of specially equipped trains to protect against acts of sabotage. General Maslin described an exercise to test the warhead security system. As a result of those exercises, he claimed in a press interview, "I became greatly concerned about a question that we had never even thought of before: What if such acts were to be undertaken by people who have worked with nuclear weapons in the past? For example, by people dismissed from our structures, social malcontents, embittered individuals?" Two additional sources – in one case the "greens" in Perm, in another, General Lebed, describe experiments to determine whether nuclear weapons depots could be penetrated. In both cases, the mock "terrorists" allegedly encountered no special difficulties in penetrating the storage sites.

PROLIFERATING KNOW-HOW

Terrorists and rogue states might also buy former Soviet weapons scientists' expertise. Senior Russian government officials admit their concern that weapons scientists, especially biological weapons specialists, are selling their expertise abroad. Russian physicists are reportedly providing consulting services to missile and nuclear energy programs in Iran and Pakistan. "Because of the deteriorating condition of the military-industrial complex in the former Soviet Union, many specialists in the field of chemical weaponry do not have enough sources of income to support their families and are ready to go anywhere to earn money," a Russian chemical weapons scientist testified. Strikes at nuclear facilities have become commonplace. The director of Chelyabinsk 70 – one of Russia's most elite nuclear weapons laboratories – killed himself, claiming he could no longer bear his inability to pay his own workers. These financial pressures on former weapons scientists pose grave risks to international security.

CHANGES IN TERRORIST OBJECTIVES AND TACTICS

Until recently, most terrorists confined themselves to relatively low-level violence. Now terrorists are becoming more violent. While the number of international incidents fell in 1996, the number of deaths increased.

Until now, in Brian Jenkins' famous words, terrorists seemed to want "a lot of people watching, not a lot of people dead." But it is increasingly clear that not all terrorists continue to be constrained by moral or political inhibitions. The *ad hoc* group of radical Islamic fundamentalists responsible for the World Trade Center bombing intended to bring the World Trade Center buildings down. Had they succeeded, the FBI estimates that some 50,000 people would have died. The terrorists made a minor error in their placement of the bomb. Nonetheless, the structural integrity of one of the twin towers and of the adjoining Vista Hotel was in jeopardy and would have collapsed spontaneously – perhaps within days of the bombing – had the buildings not been reinforced with steel supports, according to the FBI. Investigators found a cache of sodium cyanide in the bombers' warehouse. Some experts, including the sentencing judge, are convinced that cyanide was used in the bomb, but that it burned instead of vaporizing. Had it vaporized, hundreds or thousands could have been poisoned. Also in 1993, the FBI successfully thwarted a "summer of mayhem" planned by another multinational. The group was in the act of mixing up explosives when the FBI moved in, arresting eight suspects. The group was planning to bomb the UN, the Lincoln and Holland tunnels, and the Federal Plaza; and planned also to assassinate the President of Egypt, the Secretary General of the United Nations, and two members of the U.S. Congress. These groups clearly had the motivation to kill in large numbers. They failed in the first case because of a minor technical error and in the second because the FBI had been informed of the plot.

ALEXANDER LEBED

When I raised the problem of potential threat created by slackening control over compact nuclear devices, I intended, first of all, to draw public attention to this problem – with certain success. By the way, in my interview given to Interfax Agency I spoke not only on compact nuclear devices, but on safety of Russian nuclear weapons as a whole. Unfortunately, the official reaction both in Russia and the United States focused only on "nuclear suitcases." In the meantime, such issues as utilization of nuclear fuel or construction of new depositories for nuclear wastes are equally significant. As is the problem of insufficient financing of physical and technical safety of Russian civil nuclear installations that might become easy targets for terrorists.

Let us assume that Russian officials' statements saying all nuclear devices are safe and fully controlled are true. Will they be equally assuring if one says that Russian scientists who deal with technologies of production of nuclear ammunition (including compact devices) may be employed by radical regimes or may be involved in projects financed by international crime syndicates? Nowadays this threat is absolutely real.

Excerpted from Alexander Lebed's open letter to the U.S. Congress, submitted in hearings before the U.S. House Committee on Foreign Relations, October 7, 1997.

RESPONSE TO THE NEW TERRORISTS

We must attack the problem at its source, by continuing to help the Russian government secure its nuclear and chemical facilities and find alternative employment for weapons scientists. We must expedite efforts to enhance border controls to prevent smuggling of weapons of mass destruction – both at home and abroad. We must improve our ability to detect and disable nuclear, chemical, and biological weapon systems. And we must improve our intelligence abilities in support of these efforts. New legislation could expedite progress in the following areas:

Create a "nuclear emergency fund": The fund would be used in

cases where immediate assistance is requested to locate mis-
placed bombs or materials, or to secure vulnerable facilities. For
example, General Lebed requested assistance in locating atomic
demolition munitions that he claims are missing from the Russian
arsenal. Although we cannot be sure that what he says is true, it is
imperative that we investigate his claims, and that we be able to
respond to his request immediately. In addition, the fund would
be used for future "Project Sapphire" type operations. Both during
Project Sapphire and a subsequent smaller operation in Georgia,
lack of funding delayed action. In emergency situations like this,
delayed action could result in lives being needlessly lost.

**Accelerate and expand the purchase of Russian highly enriched
uranium (HEU):** The United States is buying 500 tons of highly
enriched uranium from dismantled nuclear weapons, blended
down to low enriched uranium (LEU) to be used as nuclear fuel.
The current plan is to purchase the HEU over twenty years.
Because of Russia's inability to adequately store the material, we
should negotiate with Russia to buy more HEU and to buy it
faster. Two constraints have prevented us from expediting the purchase: Russia's limited capacity for blending down its HEU, and
market concerns. One way to get around these constraints would
be to establish a "strategic nuclear fuel reserve" analogous to the
strategic petroleum reserve. All uranium (whether HEU or natural)
going into the reserve would be exempt from anti-dumping legislation and other limitations.

Expedite efforts to protect U.S. and foreign borders: The
borders of the Southern tier – including Armenia, Azerbaijan,
Kazakhstan, Russia, and Turkmenistan – are particularly perme-
able, including points of entry into Iran on the Caspian Sea.
U.S. Customs and other agencies are training personnel and
supplying enforcement agencies with tiny radiation-detection
devices the size of pocket pagers, endoscopes (for looking into gas
tanks); and other essential gear. In addition, Department of Energy
(DOE) and Customs are working together to develop new technologies for interdicting weapons of mass destruction at U.S.
points of entry. Additional funds are required to improve these
technologies and to enhance systems analysis and implementation
of advanced interception methods.

Expedite efforts to secure nuclear facilities: At the current level
of funding, DOE will require approximately four more years to
help secure nuclear materials in former Soviet states. It is entirely

MORE SMOKE THAN FIRE

Six years after the fall of the Soviet Union, loose nukes are still more smoke than fire. Journalists have chased down countless rumors, coming up with nothing concrete. Fearmongering rules because it's virtually impossible to prove a negative.

Although Lebed once had the reputation as a Russian truthteller, he himself profits from the loose nukes story, for he can argue as part of his campaign to be president that Yeltsin doesn't have control. Indeed, he admits he left office before a final audit was prepared (if one was ever done)....

William M. Arkin. "Russia's Port-a-Nukes." **The Nation.** September 29, 1997: 6-7.

unnecessary to move so slowly. With additional funding and personnel, this essential initiative could be accelerated.

Accelerate efforts to secure Russia's warheads: Poor security for Russian warheads, and deteriorating command and control may be the most significant threat to international security we currently face. Russia has requested assistance in upgrading its old-fashioned inventory and security systems. These efforts should be expedited.

Prevent "brain drain": Increasing economic desperation in Russia's closed cities poses a grave risk to international security. While most weapons scientists would never sell their expertise to terrorists or proliferant states, eventually some may become sufficiently hungry that they will sell their expertise abroad. Innovative programs run by the Departments of Energy and State help employ former weapons scientists in civilian projects that are often commercially viable. In one of these projects, scientists have developed a technique to un-irradiate milk contaminated by the Chernobyl reactor, so that local children have milk to drink that will not harm their health. In another, Russian scientists are working with Harvard Medical School on a new diphtheria vaccine. Rather than abandoning these efforts, Congress and the Administration need to work out a way to make these programs work better and faster.

READING

16

NUCLEAR ABOLITION IS THE GOAL

Jonathan Schell

Jonathan Schell is the author of Fate of the Earth *among other books. The following was excerpted from* The Nation *Magazine, a weekly journal of politics, culture and critique. An extended version of his essay was published by Metropolitan Books, spring 1998.*

■ POINTS TO CONSIDER

1. Discuss the doctrine of deterrence and its purpose during the Cold War. What does the author think of deterrence in the post-Cold War era?

2. Explain the central reason for the abolition of nuclear weapons, according to the author.

3. Summarize the chief moral question Schell poses. What is your answer?

4. Describe the circumstances, from the reading, which are favorable to nuclear abolition and explain why they are favorable.

Excerpted from Schell, Jonathan. "The Gift of Time." **The Nation.** February 2/9, 1998: 9-60. Reprinted with permission from **The Nation** Magazine © The Nation Company, L.P.

Some 35,000 nuclear weapons remain in the world. Whether nuclear weapons are held more widely and rooted more deeply is not a matter for prediction; it is a matter for choice.

Because the nuclear age and the Cold War were born at almost the same time and developed together at every point, few observers troubled at the time to distinguish clearly between the two. But now that history has unexpectedly untangled them for us, we face the one without the other, and questions in eclipse for half a century have been placed before us again. What we might call the first nuclear era, which lasted from 1945 until 1991, has come to an end, and a second nuclear era has begun. Its basic shape remains to be decided. Some 35,000 nuclear weapons remain in the world. Whether these are merely a monstrous left-over from a frightful era that has ended, and will soon follow it into history, or whether, on the contrary, they are the seeds of a new, more virulent nuclear era, in which nuclear weapons are held more widely and rooted more deeply, is not a matter for prediction; it is a matter for choice....

SAFETY FOUNDED ON TERROR

The belief that great benefit could be extracted from nuclear arms perfectly complemented the belief that their abolition was impossible. If you could not eliminate nuclear weapons, it was comforting to discover that you would not want to anyway. Abolition was doubly ruled out. Nuclear terror, once regarded as intolerable, came to be seen as the new foundation of the world's safety.

The conviction that abolition was impossible played a pivotal role in moral as well as political thinking about the nuclear question. Nuclear weapons are distinguished above all by their unparalleled destructive power. Their singularity, from a moral point of view, lies in the fact that the use of just a few would carry the user beyond every historical benchmark of indiscriminate mass slaughter. Is it necessary, fifty-three years after Hiroshima, to rehearse the basic facts? Suffice it to recall the old rule of thumb that one bomb can destroy one city. A large nuclear weapon today may possess a thousand times the explosive power of the bomb that destroyed Hiroshima – far more than enough to annihilate any city on earth. A single Trident II submarine has the capacity to deliver nearly 200 warheads, which could lay waste any nation, given the further rough rule of thumb: one boat, one nation. The use of a mere dozen nuclear weapons against, say, the dozen largest cities of the United States, Russia or China, causing tens of millions of deaths, would be a human catastrophe without parallel. The use of a few hundred nuclear weapons, not to speak of a thousand, would raise these already incomprehensible losses by orders of magnitude, leaving the imagination in the dust. Because so few weapons can kill so many people, even far-reaching disarmament proposals would leave us implicated in plans for unprecedented slaughter of innocent people. The sole measure that can free us from this burden is abolition. But abolition, during the forty or so years of the Cold War, was ruled out....

DISARMAMENT OBSTACLES REMOVED

Today, the terms of the nuclear predicament have been altered fundamentally. The barrier of impossibility has fallen. The Soviet Union has unexpectedly – almost magically – cleared itself out of the way. Gone is the murderous, implacable hostility between global rivals, which just a few years ago seemed destined to last forever; gone the totalitarian empire; and gone the obstacles to inspection that have been considered the main brake on nuclear disarmament....It is an opportunity to end the forced cohabitation with horror, the shotgun marriage with final absurdity – to snap out of the trance of the Cold War, annul the suicide pact dictated by the doctrine of deterrence and take the step that alone can free us from nuclear danger and corruption, namely, the abolition of nuclear weapons. Abolition is the great threshold. It is the logical and necessary destination because only abolition gets us out of the zone of mass slaughter, both as perpetrators and as victims.

Since the beginning of the nuclear age, it has been commonplace to say that humanity's technical achievement has outstripped its political achievement. Now the situation is reversed. The world's political achievements have raced ahead of its technical achievements. In the political realm, peace reigns, but in the technical realm hostility – indeed, threats of "mutual assured destruction" – remain the order of the day....

MORAL, POLITICAL, STRATEGIC QUESTIONS

The questions that need to be addressed are moral, political and strategic. The moral question for the United States is whether,

Cartoon by Richard Wright.

during the Cold War, we so accustomed ourselves to threatening nuclear annihilation that it became second nature to us....Can we still remember that to destroy hundreds of millions of human beings is an atrocity beyond all history? Or have we, so to speak, forgotten this before we had ever quite learned it? And have we, accordingly, adopted the strange vocation – so deeply at odds with the principles on which our nation was founded – of salesman of terror to the world?

The chief political question is whether nuclear proliferation can be stopped and reversed while the current nuclear powers declare by their actions as well as their words that they believe that nuclear bombs are indispensable instruments of power.... Although politically speaking it may in a sense be 1945 again, technically speaking it is much later than that....Back then, the nuclear club was exclusive. Now just about anyone can join....

The principal strategic question is whether the doctrine of deterrence, having been framed during the Cold War, will now be discredited as logically absurd and morally bankrupt or, on the contrary, recommended to nations all over the world as the soundest and most sensible solution to the nuclear dilemma....

It's plain that the moral, political and strategic aspects of the question are in practice tightly linked. The fundamental choice in all three areas is between, on the one hand, condemnation of nuclear weapons and their abolition and, on the other, their normalization and universalization. Normalization and universalization go naturally together. Normalization will be complete when no extraordinary external threat – and perhaps no threat at all – is thought necessary to justify building nuclear arsenals. Universalization is the natural consequence, because if possession of nuclear weapons requires no special justification, then almost any nation would be justified in having them....

ABOLITION: THE GOAL

The citizens who oppose nuclear arms are as sorely in need of fresh thinking as are the governments that possess them....The combination of comparatively low nuclear danger and high opportunity to solve the nuclear dilemma is new. During the Cold War, opposition to nuclear arms was driven by immediate, overwhelming fear – fear that ran headlong into the wall of political impossibility. Today, in sharp contrast, fear has been radically reduced....

The task is of course immense. But history has given us the gift of time – a limited time, perhaps, but enough to proceed, without haste, to scout the obstacles in our path, to weigh carefully and thoroughly the course to be followed, and then to create the structures that will carry us to the goal and keep us there. If we use the gift properly and rid the species for good of nuclear danger, we will secure the greatest of time's gifts, assurance of a human future. Of course, some will say the goal is a utopian dream of human perfection. We needn't worry. There will be more than enough sins left for everyone to commit after we have taken nuclear bombs away from ourselves....

WAITING FOR CATASTROPHE

Terror, unquestionably, is a powerful spur to action. If we wait for terror to revive, however, what price will we pay? Will it be New York City? Teheran? Berlin? Beijing? And are we sure that after such a catastrophe we would act wisely? Our reasons for acting are bound to shape the character of our action. Measures taken abruptly, after the abrupt end of fifty years of nuclear peace, possibly in an atmosphere of global suspicion, bewilderment, panic and calls for revenge, seem unlikely to be as sensible as measures adopted now, after thorough and careful discussion and preparation....

STATEMENT ON NUCLEAR WEAPONS BY INTERNATIONAL GENERALS AND ADMIRALS

It is our deep conviction that the following is urgently needed and must be undertaken now:

First, present and planned stockpiles of nuclear weapons are exceedingly large and should now be greatly cut back;

Second, remaining nuclear weapons should be gradually and transparently taken off alert, and their readiness substantially reduced both in nuclear weapon states and in *de facto* nuclear weapon states; and

Third, long-term international nuclear policy must be based on the declared principle of continuous, complete and irrevocable elimination of nuclear weapons.

Excerpted from the "Statement on Nuclear Weapons by International Generals and Admirals" signed by Generals and Admirals from 17 countries.

To succeed in the task would, by securing human survival through human resolve and action, go far toward restoring our faith, so badly shaken in this century, in our capacity to make use of the amazing products of our hands and minds for our benefit rather than our destruction. It would bring undying honor to those who carried it to fulfillment and to their generation. It would have the character not of a desperate expedient resorted to under pressure of terror but of a tremendous free act, following upon calm public deliberation in every nation – among all humankind. In a way, it would be the foundation of humankind....

READING

17

NUCLEAR DETERRENTS REMAIN JUSTIFIED

Walter B. Slocombe

Walter B. Slocombe is the Under Secretary of Defense for Policy of the United States Defense Department.

■ POINTS TO CONSIDER

1. Briefly summarize the utility of nuclear weapons in the Cold War period, according to Slocombe.

2. According to the author, nuclear weapons maintain their utility even though the Soviet Empire, our main Cold War rival, disintegrated in 1990. Why are the weapons useful, even necessary for the author?

3. How does the author respond to the argument that having nuclear weapons causes other nations to seek their own arsenals?

4. Discuss some of the key barriers to nuclear abolition.

Excerpted from the testimony of Walter B. Slocombe before the Subcommittee on International Security, Proliferation and Federal Services of the U.S. Senate Committee on Governmental Affairs, February 12, 1997.

***The existence of nuclear weapons continues to serve
as a damper on the resort to the use of force.***

Nuclear deterrence has been the subject of much debate over
the decades, and, appropriately, this debate has been resumed
after the end of the Cold War. Most recently, the nuclear question
has been given prominence by respected individuals and committees who advocate a radical change – setting as a policy goal the
complete abolition of nuclear weapons.

For the foreseeable future, we will continue to need a reliable
and flexible nuclear deterrent – survivable against the most
aggressive attack, under highly confident constitutional command
and control, and assured in its safety against both accident and
unauthorized use.

We will need such a force because nuclear deterrence – far
from being made wholly obsolete – remains an essential ultimate
assurance against the gravest of threats.

NUCLEAR DETERRENCE: THE COLD WAR

Because the past has lessons for the future, let me review briefly
how our nuclear forces have strengthened our security. First, they
provided a principal means by which the United States deterred
conventional and nuclear aggression by the Soviet Union and
Warsaw Pact Nations against itself and its allies. Second, the
extension of the U.S. nuclear umbrella allowed many of our allies
to forego their own nuclear weapons, even though they had the
technological know-how to develop them. Third, although the
East-West competition spilled over into numerous regional conflicts during the Cold War, the nuclear capabilities possessed by
the superpowers instilled caution, lest the United States and the
Soviet Union be brought into direct, and possibly nuclear, con-
frontation.

It is a remarkable fact that for almost half a century, the U.S.
and its allies faced the USSR and its coerced auxiliaries in a division over ideology, power, culture, and the very definition of
man, the state, and the world, and did so armed to the greatest
extent huge sacrifice would afford, and yet did not fight a large-
scale war.

Some argued, even in the Cold War, that the danger of a
nuclear holocaust was so great that the risk of possessing these

115

weapons far outweighed their benefits. I do not agree. Nuclear deterrence helped buy us time, time for internal forces of upheaval and decay to rend the Soviet Union and the Warsaw Pact Nations and bring about the end of the Cold War.

POST-COLD WAR NUCLEAR DETERRENCE

But the Cold War is over, and it is important to recognize the great degree to which our nuclear deterrence and indeed that of Russia has been transformed from that period. The role of nuclear weapons in our defense posture has diminished – we welcome this trend and expect it will continue in the future. U.S. spending on strategic forces has declined dramatically from Cold War levels – from 24 percent of the total Department of Defense (DOD) budget in the mid-1960s, to seven percent in 1991, to less than three percent today. Russian spending on strategic forces has also declined substantially.

Nor is the nonproliferation picture all bleak. No nation has openly joined the nuclear club since China in 1964. There are only three unacknowledged nuclear powers. South Africa has abandoned its capability, as Ukraine, Belarus and Kazakhstan have theirs. Argentina and Brazil have renounced the option, as Sweden and Canada did long ago. North Korea's program is frozen. Iraq is under a special and highly intrusive United Nations Special Commission (UNSCOM) regime. The vast majority of countries support a permanent Nonproliferation Treaty – mostly a benefit which non-nuclear countries confer on one another, not a favor they do for the nuclear powers. We have negotiated an end to nuclear testing.

WHY NUCLEAR DETERRENCE?

The question, however, is rightly asked: Granted all these reductions, with the end of the Cold War, why do we continue to maintain a nuclear deterrence at all?

First, Russia has made great progress and we do not regard it as a potential military threat under its present, or any reasonably foreseeable government. We wisely invest substantially in the Cooperative Threat Reduction program, in future arms control – and we share with the current Russian leadership (and most of their opponents) a determination not to let our relations return to a state of hostility in which these weapons would be a threat.

116

Cartoon by Mike Shelton. Reprinted with permission, **King Feature Syndicate.**

All that said, Russia continues to possess substantial strategic forces and an even larger stockpile of tactical nuclear weapons. And because of deterioration in its conventional military capabilities, Russia may be placing even more importance and reliance on its nuclear forces. We cannot be so certain of future Russian politics as to ignore the possibility that we would need again to deter the Russian nuclear force.

Second, even if we could ignore the Russian nuclear arsenal entirely, there are unfortunately a range of other potential threats to which nuclear weapons are a deterrent. One cannot survey the list of rogue states with potential Weapons of Mass Destruction (WMD) programs and conclude otherwise. I do not, by the way, regard such states as undeterrable, either in the long-run sense of the incentives to acquire WMD capability, or the short-run sense of incentives to use such a capability. Indeed, the knowledge that the U.S. has a powerful and ready nuclear capability is, I believe, a significant deterrent to proliferators to even contemplate the use of WMD. That this is so will, I think, be clear if one thinks about the proliferation incentives that would be presented to the Kaddafis and Kim-Chong-Ils of the world if the U.S. did not have a reliable and flexible nuclear capability.

In view of this, it would be irresponsible to dismantle the well-established – and much reduced – system of deterrence before new and reliable systems for preserving stability are in place.

117

OTHERS SEEK THEIR OWN

What about the argument that our weapons promote proliferation, that states seek to acquire nuclear weapons in response to possession by nuclear weapons states? A more compelling case to me is that proliferant states acquire nuclear weapons not because we have them but for reasons of their own – to counter regional adversaries, to further regional ambitions, and to enhance their status among their neighbors. And, insofar as our nuclear capability is an issue, if a successful proliferator knew he would not face a nuclear response by the U.S., it would scarcely reduce his incentives to acquire a WMD capability.

Some people claim that once proliferation does occur, U.S. nuclear forces lack any utility in deterring rogue leaders from using nuclear weapons because those leaders will not regard the costs, even of nuclear retaliation, as sufficiently great. But experience suggests that few dictators are indifferent to the preservation of key instruments of state control, or to the survival of their own regimes (or, indeed, their own persons). Thus, I believe the reverse is true – our nuclear capabilities are more likely to give pause to potential rogue proliferants than encourage them.

ABOLITION IS IMPRACTICAL

There is no reasonable prospect that all the declared and *de facto* nuclear powers will agree in the near term to give up all their nuclear weapons. And as long as one such state refuses to do so, it will be necessary for us to retain a nuclear force of our own. If the nuclear powers were, nevertheless, to accept abolition, then we would require – and the Congress would rightly demand – a verification regime of extraordinary rigor and intrusiveness. This would have to go far beyond any currently in existence or even under contemplation. It would have to include not merely a system of verification, but what the "international generals' statement" calls "an agreed procedure for forcible international intervention and interruption of current efforts in a certain and timely fashion." Such a regime would have to continue to be effective in the midst of a prolonged and grave crisis – even during a war – between potentially nuclear-capable powers. For in such a crisis, the first question for all involved would be that of whether – or when – to start a clandestine nuclear program. For the knowledge of how to build nuclear weapons cannot be abolished.

Finally, we who are charged with responsibility for national security and national defense must recall that we are not only seeking to avert nuclear war – we are seeking to avert major conventional war, as well. As I indicated earlier, during the Cold War nuclear weapons played a stabilizing role in that they made the resort to military force less likely. The world is still heavily armed with advanced conventional weapons and will increasingly be so armed with weapons of mass destruction. The existence of nuclear weapons continues to serve as a damper on the resort to the use of force.

SUMMARY

Our objective is a safe, stable world. But we must develop our national security policy with the understanding that nuclear weapons and the underlying technical knowledge cannot be disinvented whether or not the U.S. retains its weapons. We will maintain a smaller nuclear force as a "hedge" against a future that is uncertain and in a world in which substantial nuclear arsenals remain.

EXAMINING COUNTERPOINTS

This activity may be used as an individualized study guide for students in libraries and resource centers or as a discussion catalyst in small group and classroom discussions.

The Point

The 1998 nuclear showdown between India and Pakistan demonstrates that the world is not safe for disarmament. Since the world is no longer dotted with a few nuclear elites, the threat of nuclear attack, from nation states and terrorist groups, is even greater than during the Cold War. Maintaining a nuclear arsenal is the best way to deter nuclear-capable parties from intimidation and attack.

The Counterpoint

The 1998 nuclear showdown between India and Pakistan determines the final judgment of nuclear weapons. Considering the great strain they place on resources in their development and maintenance (which is particularly burdensome to developing countries such as India and Pakistan) and the great price the world will pay in human life in the event of war or terrorist attack, the global community must make every effort to eliminate nuclear weapons.

Guidelines

Part A

Examine the counterpoints above and then consider the following questions:

1. Do you agree more with the point or counterpoint? Why?

2. Which reading in this book best illustrates the point?

3. Which reading best illustrates the counterpoint?

4. Do any cartoons in this book illustrate the meaning of the point or counterpoint arguments? Which ones and why?

Part B

Social issues are usually complex, but often problems become oversimplified in political debates and discussions. Usually a polarized version of social conflict does not adequately represent the diversity of views that surround social conflicts. Examine the counterpoints. Then write down possible interpretations of this issue other than the two arguments stated in the counterpoints.

CHAPTER 4

WEAPONS OF MASS DESTRUCTION: IDEAS IN CONFLICT

READING

18

CRACKING DOWN ON SMUGGLING: HALTING THE SPREAD OF WEAPONS OF MASS DESTRUCTION

Thomas E. McNamara

Thomas E. McNamara is the Assistant Secretary of State for Political-Military Affairs under the Department of State.

■ **POINTS TO CONSIDER**

1. Describe how the breakup of the Former Soviet Union affects efforts to control nuclear proliferation.

2. What does the author emphasize as the threat to efforts to halt the spread of nuclear weapons?

3. Explain one way to inhibit smuggling.

4. Contrast the export control system in Russia with that of the Former Soviet Union.

Excerpted from the testimony of Thomas E. McNamara before the Permanent Subcommittee on Investigations of the U.S. Senate Committee on Governmental Affairs, March 22, 1996.

Nuclear smuggling constitutes a direct threat to our efforts to halt the spread of nuclear weapons.

A small quantity of plutonium – roughly an amount the size of a softball – is sufficient to destroy a city. And, the plutonium and uranium we have freed from nuclear weapons will last for thousands of years. It is thus imperative that we continue our efforts, in cooperation with Russia and other countries, to secure the nuclear materials, protect nuclear technology, and redirect weapons skills to peaceful pursuits.

CHANGING GEO-POLITICAL CLIMATE

The breakup of the Soviet Empire radically changed the proliferation landscape. Three additional states emerged with nuclear weapons on their territories. The Soviet system for protecting and controlling nuclear materials, designed to work within a totalitarian police state, went the way of the Former Soviet Union (FSU). As the nations of the FSU face the transition to more democratic forms of government, they are confronted with the much more complex task of protecting nuclear materials within free societies. Finally, the combination of extreme economic dislocation and the emergence of organized crime that has afflicted the states of the FSU increased both the temptation and the potential means to divert nuclear material.

We recognized from the start that this problem cannot be attacked on only one front. We decided to attack this problem on several fronts, and to devise a layered defense against the threat. We have sought to control the sources of supply of nuclear materials as well as technology and items used in the production or use of special nuclear materials; to reduce demand; to ease the economic dislocations that followed the breakup of the Soviet Union; and to strengthen law enforcement and intelligence capabilities needed if the security of the materials is breached.

From the beginning, therefore, we have concentrated our efforts on securing nuclear weapons, nuclear materials, and requisite skills to design such weapons at their source.

SMUGGLING CONTROL

As long as any nuclear material remains at risk, and the possible temptation to sell it remains, we must continue to refine our tools for fighting the threat of illicit trafficking.

The most visible symptom of this risk, of illicit transfers of nuclear material, are the reported cases of smuggling by individuals or small groups whose chief goal is monetary gain.

Nuclear smuggling constitutes a direct threat to our efforts to halt the spread of nuclear weapons. Trafficking in nuclear material bypasses key elements of the international regime to halt nuclear proliferation. The regime operates on the assumption that states can and will control sensitive materials. Nuclear trafficking on the other hand is largely the act of unauthorized individuals outside national control, who have found some gap in the nuclear material security systems of states.

National and international mechanisms to control proliferation assume that the single most important technical step in developing nuclear weapons is to acquire nuclear weapons usable material. Manufacture of this material requires the investment of hundreds of millions of dollars and years of sophisticated engineering. Smuggling of such material bypasses the time and the cost, and short-circuits the principal technical barrier to nuclear proliferation.

APATHY IS TOO COSTLY

We have no evidence that a transaction of this kind has yet occurred. Indeed, in the area of the security of nuclear weapons, we are confident that such a breakdown in security is less likely, but we are continuing our support for safe and secure transport and storage of nuclear weapons. However, we cannot afford to be complacent. We know nuclear weapons grade material is at risk. We know that there are covert networks to acquire sensitive technology for weapons of mass destruction (WMD). And we know that criminals have obtained at least small quantities of nuclear material in the past few years. The international community clearly sees this threat and is taking the steps necessary to forestall it.

Nuclear smuggling is not like other kinds of illegal trafficking. We cannot afford to have even a single case of successful smuggling of enough nuclear material for a weapon. We cannot realistically expect any strategy based only on law enforcement and interdiction to be one hundred percent effective. Thus, anti-smuggling initiatives have necessarily been only a part of our response to the changing world situation.

Most of the early reported cases were transparent scams involving inert substances or radioactive materials without weapons applications. Nonetheless, despite the sensationalism surrounding these cases, we recognized the nature of the problem and the need to combat it on many fronts.

DEMAND SIDE INTERVENTION

We have not forgotten about the demand side of the equation. There will always be a risk of nuclear smuggling as long as proliferators are prepared to offer cash for illegal nuclear goods. We have energized our significant intelligence capabilities to track the covert procurement efforts of rogue states. We share information with the states affected by these procurement networks to frustrate them. We provide assistance to the UN Special Commission and the International Atomic Energy Agency in their efforts to tear out Iraq's covert weapons of mass destruction programs at the root. And, we are assisting financially and technically new effort to develop safeguard methods to detect clandestine nuclear activities. At the same time, we continue our diplomatic efforts to persuade countries of proliferation concern to halt their programs for WMD development.

RUSSIA: DEVELOPING EXPORT CONTROLS

Export controls are the initial barrier between suppliers and unauthorized recipients, and thus effectively inhibit demand. The export control system inherited by Russian and the newly independent states (NIS) was not designed to cope with the current freedom of or volume of trade. Since sensitive materials were never allowed to be exported without the express consent of the centralized Soviet government, the problem of inspection and proper identification of products that bypassed the centralized system was not a problem which the Soviet export control system had to deal with. The development of an export control system which is capable of making informed decisions about license applications as well as identifying commodities in transit for interdiction purposes has, therefore, been a focus for U.S.-Russian and U.S.-NIS cooperation. The export control system emerging from this cooperation will be much more adept at preventing proliferation of technology and commodities useful in nuclear weapons, the development of nuclear weapons, and unsafeguarded fuel cycle activities.

STRATEGY AGAINST TERRORISTS

The threats to the well-being of society posed by protracted insurgencies that employ terrorism to achieve their political objectives must be dealt with by governmental law enforcement and military measures, intelligence and covert operations, international cooperation, and international sanctions. These coercive measures, however, while essential, are not sufficient. To fully confront this problem, an additional equal option is necessary: the complementary strategy of conciliation. The application of these two integral approaches are the most effective ways for governments to resolve terrorist-type rebellions in the long-term. This is also the ideal solution favored by democratic governments.

Excerpted from the testimony of Joshua Sinai before the U.S. House of Representatives Permanent Select Committee on Intelligence, Seminar held by CRS, December 7, 1995.

UNITED STATES' INTEREST

The countries that harbor the remnants of the Soviet nuclear infrastructure have transitional economies and are hampered in their ability to devote resources, and in some cases expertise, to the protection of nuclear material. It is clearly in our national interest to expand the effort and the necessary funds to assure that this material is protected at its source.

We need to energize other states and the international community to take a number of steps to further reduce the danger of nuclear trafficking. We continue to work with our partners to foster international cooperation to ensure the security of nuclear materials and to combat nuclear smuggling.

READING

19

REFORMING THE ETHICS OF EXPORT: HALTING THE SPREAD OF WEAPONS OF MASS DESTRUCTION

Gary Milhollin

Gary Milhollin is a professor at the University of Wisconsin School of Law and director of the Wisconsin Project on Nuclear Arms Control.

■ POINTS TO CONSIDER

1. Evaluate the author's point concerning the threat of "rogue nations."

2. Summarize the meaning of "constructive engagement" as a policy. What is the author's point about the value of this type of policy?

3. What action does Milhollin identify as "worse than smuggling" in the effort to halt the spread of weapons of mass destruction?

4. Analyze the author's reference to United States' deals with North Korea. What is he trying to say about nuclear nonproliferation or about the U.S. role in such efforts?

Excerpted from the testimony of Gary Milhollin before the Permanent Subcommittee on Investigations of the U.S. Senate Committee on Governmental Affairs, March 20, 1996.

Realize that there is something worse than smuggling: It is deliberate, over-the-table supply, which includes training, spare parts and technical back-up.

I would like to begin with the idea of "rogue nations" – now thought to include Iran, Iraq, Libya and North Korea. This is a new term that the Clinton Administration has coined to define the proliferation problem, and to restrict it to these four countries. Unfortunately, it ignores a lot of proliferation.

CHINA

China is a very serious proliferation threat. As far as we know, China is the only country that still targets American cities with nuclear warheads. It is also testing thermonuclear warheads to miniaturize them, so they will fit on new missiles capable of reaching the United States. And Chinese exports continue to fuel proliferation in both Iran and Pakistan. China is not a member of the Nuclear Suppliers Group, the Missile Technology Control Regime or the Australia Group – the agreements that seek to control the sale of the means to make nuclear weapons, chemical weapons and the missiles to deliver them. Unless China stops testing nuclear weapons and stops selling nuclear and missile technology to other countries, the proliferation problem will be impossible to solve. China supplied nuclear technology to Algeria, Iran, Iraq and Syria, and missile technology to Pakistan, Saudi Arabia and Syria. Since 1994, China has supplied missile components and poison gas ingredients to Iran, and sold Pakistan missile components and magnets for producing nuclear weapon material.

SOUTH ASIA

The magnets have refocused public attention on South Asia, where the nuclear threat is growing. Pakistan has already made around a dozen warheads and the magnets will boost its ability to make more; India possesses at least a score of warheads. Both countries built their programs with outside help. India's plutonium-producing reactors are copied from Canadian designs and operated with material from China, Norway and Russia. Pakistan's plants for producing weapons-grade uranium are built from European designs and outfitted with equipment from Germany and Switzerland. India's short-range missile uses rocket motors taken from a Soviet-supplied surface-to-air missile, and India's medium-range missile uses a first stage copied from a U.S. satellite launcher, a second stage based on the Soviet surface-to-air missile, and a guidance system developed with help from the German space agency. Pakistan's missiles, of course, come from China. If you look behind the nuclear and missile programs of either India or Pakistan, you will see that practically nothing is home-grown. And both India and Pakistan are still shopping.

ROGUE NATIONS

The idea that we only need to worry about four "rogue nations" is wrong. China, India and Pakistan are active proliferants – and their behavior is getting worse. The new strategy of confining the problem to the four "rogues" seems to be a move by the Administration to boost U.S. exports. Because the United States does not trade with the rogues anyway, confining the problem to them allows American companies to sell to everybody else. The late Commerce Secretary Ron Brown, for example, gave a trade promotion speech in 1995 at the Indian Institute of Science in Bangalore, one of India's main rocket research sites. It is developing rockets big enough to carry nuclear warheads throughout Asia and eventually the world. One can only wonder what Secretary Brown hoped to sell to this customer.

Iran, Iraq, Libya and North Korea are all members of the Nuclear Nonproliferation Treaty. Yet, they are proliferation threats. Getting countries to join the Treaty, and getting the Treaty extended, doesn't mean much unless the Treaty has some teeth. Does it? China joined in 1992, but broke Article III and probably Article I by exporting the ring magnets to Pakistan. Article III prohibits such exports except under international inspection – which China did not require – and Article I prohibits assistance that helps a country like Pakistan make nuclear weapons. It seems clear that Pakistan bought the magnets to make nuclear weapons. But has anyone complained?

This silence has a precedent. It is the same American silence that greeted the Iraqis when they were caught trying to smuggle nuclear weapons triggers out of the United States before the Gulf War. Rather than apply sanctions, or even complain publicly about Iraq's violation of the Treaty, the State Department chose "constructive engagement." It would be better to maintain our influence with Saddam Hussein through trade. By selling him what he wanted, we would bring Saddam into the mainstream of nations. Sanctions would only hurt American exporters and allow the Europeans and the Japanese to get all the business. We now know what that strategy produced. We were lucky. If Saddam had not been foolish enough to invade Kuwait, we would be facing a nuclear-armed Iraq with its shadow over most of the world's oil supply. And Iraq would have made it to the bomb while staying in the Nonproliferation Treaty.

LEGAL, NOT ILLICIT MEANS

The Iraqi threat has not gone away. Before the Gulf War, Iraq filled 166 bombs and 25 missile warheads with anthrax, botulinum and alfatoxin – all deadly germ warfare agents – and tested missile warheads filled with VX, the most lethal form of nerve gas. All of this was completely unknown to our troops, and was still unknown to the UN inspectors until 1995, more than four years after the War. This shows that mass destruction weapons can be built in secret, maintained in secret, and be ready to inflict deadly surprises on both troops and civilians. We don't know what other surprises Saddam Hussein may be hiding, but the chances are that he is still hiding something.

Iraq is still much closer to the bomb than Iran. Iraq has the know-how it gained before the Gulf War and it has not disbanded its nuclear weapon teams. Because of its experience, Iraq would be able to convert smuggled material to a usable weapon much faster than Iran would. We also know that Iraq is still shopping. Recently, missile guidance components on their way to Iraq from Russia were seized in Jordan, and similar components were pulled out of the Tigris River by UN inspectors. I have provided the Subcommittee with a graphic from the *New York Times* based on data that our project put together. The data show the astonishing amount of help Iraq got from foreign suppliers before the Gulf War, mostly from Germany and Switzerland.

I would like to emphasize that almost all of this equipment was shipped legally – in accordance with the export control laws of the time. Today, export laws are even weaker than they were before the Gulf War. Realize that there is something worse than smuggling: It is deliberate, over-the-table supply, which includes training, spare parts and technical back-up.

NEED FOR GLOBAL POLICY

The Russians love to cite the U.S. reactor deal with North Korea. If America can give two big reactors to North Korea, they say, why can't Russia sell the same kind of reactors to Iran? Is Iran less reliable than North Korea? Iran has not broken the Nonproliferation Treaty, but North Korea has. In fact, North Korea is the first country in violation of the Nonproliferation Treaty ever to get a reactor with America's blessing. The U.S. deal with North Korea has made it impossible to stop the Russian reactor deal with Iran.

The Clinton Administration is following the same policy toward China today that the Bush Administration followed toward Iraq before the Gulf War: "Hold your nose and export." This is also the same policy that our European allies are following toward Iran – a policy that we officially deplore. But if we hold our noses and trade with China, why can't the Europeans and the Russians hold their noses and trade with Iran?

Only a global policy will work – a policy that opposes proliferation everywhere. And it must be a policy that puts security above profits. If the United States puts profits first, so will everyone else. But we cannot sell everything to everybody, except four "rogue" countries, and expect the world to think we are serious about curbing proliferation. One person's rogue is another person's valued customer.

MILITARY ACTION AGAINST TERRORISTS: THE POINT

William J. Clinton

William J. Clinton is the 42nd President of the United States. On August 20, 1998, the President ordered air strikes on a commercial factory in Khartoum, Sudan, and encampments in Afghanistan. The air strikes were controversial – they came in the midst of an embarrassing personal scandal for the President. Also, doubts were raised concerning the justification for strikes (see next reading).

■ **POINTS TO CONSIDER**

1. Why does President Clinton give this address?

2. According to Clinton, what role does Osama bin Ladin have in this international conflict? Do you believe the President's characterization?

3. Comment on the tone of the reading.

4. Assess the effectiveness of the speech. Does it convince you of the need for bombings?

Excerpted from the address to the nation from President William J. Clinton, August 20, 1998.

Their mission is murder, and their history is bloody.

Today I ordered our armed forces to strike at terrorist-related facilities in Afghanistan and Sudan because of the imminent threat they presented to our national security. I want to speak with you about the objective of this action and why it was necessary.

TARGET OF TERROR

Our target was terror. Our mission was clear: to strike at the network of radical groups affiliated with and funded by Osama bin Ladin, perhaps the preeminent organizer and financier of international terrorism in the world today.

The groups associated with him come from diverse places but share a hatred for democracy, a fanatical glorification of violence, and a horrible distortion of their religion, to justify the murder of innocents. They have made the United States their adversary precisely because of what we stand for and what we stand against.

A few months ago and again this week, bin Ladin publicly vowed to wage a terrorist war against America, saying – and I quote – "We do not differentiate between those dressed in military uniforms and civilians. They're all targets."

MISSION OF MURDER

Their mission is murder, and their history is bloody. In recent years they killed American, Belgian, and Pakistani peacekeepers in Somalia. They plotted to assassinate the President of Egypt and the Pope. They planned to bomb six United States 747s over the Pacific. They bombed the Egyptian Embassy in Pakistan. They gunned down German tourists in Egypt.

The most recent terrorist events are fresh in our memory. Two weeks ago, 12 Americans and nearly 300 Kenyans and Tanzanians lost their lives and another 5,000 were wounded when our embassies in Nairobi and Dar es Salaam were bombed. There is convincing information from our intelligence community that the bin Ladin terrorist network was responsible for these bombings. Based on this information, we have high confidence that these bombings were planned, financed, and carried out by the organization bin Ladin leads.

Cartoon by Steve Benson. Reprinted with permission, **UFS.**

DIPLOMACY FALLS SHORT

America has battled terrorism for many years. Where possible, we've used law enforcement and diplomatic tools to wage the fight. The long arm of American law has reached out around the world and brought to trial those guilty of attacks in New York, in Virginia, and in the Pacific. We have quietly disrupted terrorist groups and foiled their plots. We have isolated countries that practice terrorism. We've worked to build an international coalition against terror. But there have been and will be times when law enforcement and diplomatic tools are simply not enough, when our very national security is challenged, and when we must take extraordinary steps to protect the safety of our citizens.

With compelling evidence that the bin Ladin network of terrorist groups was planning to mount further attacks against Americans and other freedom-loving people, I decided America must act. And so this morning, based on the unanimous recommendations of my national security team, I ordered our Armed Forces to take action to counter an immediate threat from the bin Ladin network.

AFGHANISTAN, SUDAN

Earlier today, the United States carried out simultaneous strikes against terrorist facilities and infrastructure in Afghanistan. Our forces targeted one of the most active terrorist bases in the world.

OSAMA BIN LADIN

Bin Ladin, the youngest son of a wealthy Saudi business-man, developed a worldwide organization in the 1970s to recruit Muslim terrorists for the war against the Soviets in Afghanistan. In 1988, he formed a network devoted to terror and subversion. He returned to his home in Saudi Arabia in 1989, but the Government of Saudi Arabia expelled him the following year for his continued support of terrorist groups.

Excerpted from "Fact Sheet: Osama bin Ladin," as released by the Coordinator for Counterterrorism, Department of State, August, 21, 1998.

It contained key elements of the bin Ladin network's infrastructure and has served as a training camp for literally thousands of terrorists from around the globe. We have reason to believe that a gathering of key terrorist leaders was to take place there today, thus underscoring the urgency of our actions. Our forces also attacked a factory in Sudan associated with the bin Ladin network. The factory was involved in the production of materials for chemical weapons.

The United States does not take this action lightly. Afghanistan and Sudan have been warned for years to stop harboring and supporting these terrorist groups. But countries that persistently host terrorists have no right to be safe havens.

Let me express my gratitude to our intelligence and law enforcement agencies for their hard, good work. And let me express my pride in our armed forces, who carried out this mission while making every possible effort to minimize the loss of innocent life.

I want you to understand, I want the world to understand that our actions today were not aimed against Islam, the faith of hundreds of millions of good, peace-loving people all around the world, including the United States. No religion condones the murder of innocent men, women and children. But our actions were aimed at fanatics and killers who wrap murder in the cloak of righteousness and, in so doing, profane the great religion in whose name they claim to act.

BATTLE OF ENDURANCE

My fellow Americans, our battle against terrorism did not begin with the bombing of our embassies in Africa, nor will it end with today's strike. It will require strength, courage and endurance. We will not yield to this threat. We will meet it no matter how long it may take. This will be a long, ongoing struggle between freedom and fanaticism, between the rule of law and terrorism. We must be prepared to do all that we can for as long as we must. America is and will remain a target of terrorists precisely because we are leaders; because we act to advance peace, democracy and basic human values; because we're the most open society on earth; and because, as we have shown yet again, we take an uncompromising stand against terrorism.

But of this I am also sure; the risks from inaction to America and the world would be far greater than from action, for that would embolden our enemies, leaving their ability and their willingness to strike us intact. In this case, we knew before our attack that these groups already had planned further actions against us and others.

DETERMINATION AGAINST TERROR

I want to reiterate: The United States wants peace, not conflict. We want to lift lives around the world, not take them. We have worked for peace in Bosnia, in Northern Ireland, in Haiti, in the Middle East and elsewhere, but in this day, no campaign for peace can succeed without a determination to fight terrorism.

Let our actions today send this message loud and clear: There are no expendable American targets. There will be no sanctuary for terrorists. We will defend our people, our interests and our values. We will help people of all faiths in all parts of the world who want to live free of fear and violence. We will persist and we will prevail.

Thank you, God bless you, and may God bless our country.

READING

21

MILITARY ACTION AGAINST TERRORISTS: THE COUNTERPOINT

Doug Bandow

Doug Bandow is a syndicated columnist. He wrote the following for the Copley News Service.

■ POINTS TO CONSIDER

1. What is the important lesson, according to Bandow, of the terrorist bombings in Kenya and Tanzania?

2. Examine the author's claim that terrorism is often a "rational response."

3. Summarize Bandow's examples of U.S. hypocrisy in foreign policy. Do you agree that these are hypocrisies?

4. Examine and explain the statement, "The best defense is to give no offense."

Bandow, Doug. "The High Price of Foreign Intervention." **Conservative Chronicle.** September 2, 1998. Reprinted with permission of **Copley News Service.**

Even a superpower like the United States cannot intervene abroad without cost. Unfortunately, the price of attempting to run the world is ruined buildings and mangled bodies.

The tragic bombing of two U.S. embassies in Africa obviously illustrates the danger of representing America abroad. But there is another, more important lesson. Even a superpower like the United States cannot intervene abroad without cost. Unfortunately, the price of attempting to run the world is ruined buildings and mangled bodies.

Even President Clinton acknowledged the connection in his radio address – though, of course, he didn't admit responsibility. He argued: "Americans are targets of terrorism, in part, because we have unique leadership responsibilities in the world, because we act to advance peace and democracy." To pull back would exhibit weakness, he claimed, so we have no choice but to "continue to take the fight to terrorists."

U.S. HAS CHOICE

However, the United States doesn't "have" leadership responsibilities; it chooses leadership responsibilities. Few duties are absolute. We live in a world in which almost every other country wants America to defend, subsidize, support or otherwise aid them. If the definition of leadership responsibilities was what other nations desired, Washington would do, well, what it is doing now – defending, subsidizing, supporting and aiding virtually every other state.

But Washington should consider costs, including the catastrophic human toll from terrorism, before deciding what responsibilities to fulfill. Terrorists kill for a cause. The bombers in Kenya and Tanzania were almost certainly retaliating for particular U.S. policies. Those who attacked the American military base in Dhahran, Saudi Arabia, and the World Trade Center in New York were similarly motivated.

RATIONAL RESPONSE

Of course, terrorism is a monstrous act. But it is a sadly rational response, since it is the only effective weapon for weak states or small groups confronting the world's dominant power. While the

Cartoon by Robert Gorrell. Reprinted with permission, **Creators Syndicate, Inc.**

United States should deal forcefully with terrorist threats and retaliate when possible, Americans should not delude themselves that Washington is suffering only because it is busy promoting, as the President claimed, "peace and democracy" around the globe.

By stationing U.S. soldiers in Saudi Arabia, for instance, Washington is buttressing a totalitarian government. The Saudi royal family loots the economy, suppresses political opposition and bans non-Muslim religions. Washington may view its support as a necessary bit of Realpolitik. But America is suppressing, not aiding democracy.

For that reason Mohammed Masari, a Saudi exile, terms U.S. forces "legitimate targets." Another critic of the Saudi regime, Osama bin Laden, says that "Muslims burn with anger at America." They are at war with Riyadh, Saudi Arabia, and Washington is openly siding with their enemies. The United States has made itself a target.

BACKLASH IS NOT SURPRISING

The bombings of the American Embassy and Marine Corps barracks in Lebanon in 1983 were similar. In the name of "peace and democracy," the United States backed the ruling Christian faction against Muslim groups in what was a full-scale civil war. Washington even used its fleet to bombard Druze villages, filled

ADMINISTRATION INCOMPETENCIES

Here's the forecast today for Milwaukee: Warm and sunny, with a 20 percent chance of cruise missiles. The Aldrich Chemical Company, you see, is located there, and it makes a chemical known as EMPTA. This is the same compound that the Clinton Administration says was being manufactured in a so-called pharmaceutical plant in Sudan, a chemical that supposedly has no conceivable use except in nerve gas. If the Sudanese can't be trusted with this stuff, can cheese-heads?

When you start firing volleys of cruise missiles at a target inside a sovereign nation, you had better have an awfully good excuse. But in the time since the Khartoum factory was blown to bits, the Clinton Administration has done a thoroughly incompetent job of defending its action....

Stephen Chapman. "The Crumbling U.S. Case Against Sudan." **Conservative Chronicle.** September 9, 1998.

with people who had never bothered America. That Muslims responded violently was tragic, but should not have surprised U.S. policy-makers.

The Mideast is the front of much terrorism against America. Washington has long aided Israel and ignored the plight of displaced Palestinians. The United States backed the Shah's brutal dictatorship in Iran and continues to support Saudi Arabia and the other Gulf autocracies. The war against Iraq also fanned passions.

HYPOCRISY

The embers glow in other regions. Somalia demonstrated that not everyone wants to be "saved" by Washington. American policy-makers publicly dismiss democracy when Islamic fundamentalists win elections in Algeria, Egypt, Jordan and Turkey.

Hypocrisy in the Balkans – condemning ethnic cleansing by Serbs while ignoring it by Croats – has left many people believing the United States stands for something other than "peace and democracy." Arrogant demands by Washington rankle in China, Russia, and elsewhere.

For good reason, then, Charles Englehart of Kroll-Ogara, a business security firm, says that "there are a whole lot of people who hate America."

Of course, popularity is not necessarily a sign of being right. But U.S. policy is often glaringly wrong. Even when it isn't, Washington still needs to decide whether U.S. interests are important enough to warrant intervention. And that requires remembering that intervention begets terrorism.

PRICE IS TOO HIGH

The cost of terrorism is high enough today. As weapons of mass destruction spread, however, the price could become staggering. Imagine the use of biological, chemical or nuclear weapons at the World Trade Center. As potential terrorists' power grows, intervening for marginal international gains will become increasingly foolish.

By all means, Washington should combat terrorism. But the best defense is to give no offense. The twin bombings in East Africa offer two more reasons for not promiscuously meddling in overseas conflicts that don't concern the United States. It is almost always innocent victims — embassy personnel and foreign civilians – rather than Washington policy-makers who pay the terrorists' hideous bill.

READING

22

CONTAINING IRAQ: THE POINT

Richard Perle

Richard Perle is a resident fellow at the American Enterprise Institute for Public Policy Research, 1150 17th St., N.W., Washington, D.C. 20036. The American Enterprise Institute sponsors research on government policy, politics and economy. The Institute emphasizes limited government and private enterprise.

■ POINTS TO CONSIDER

1. Who does the author hold responsible for the U.S./Iraqi conflict? Why?

2. Describe Perle's assessment of current U.S. policy toward Iraq.

3. Discuss the effects of sanctions, according to the author.

4. Summarize the ten policy recommendations Perle gives.

Excerpted from the testimony of Richard Perle before the U.S. Senate Committee on Foreign Relations and the U.S. Senate Committee on Energy and Natural Resource, May 21, 1998.

*More than six years after his defeat in Desert Storm,
Saddam Hussein is outsmarting, outmaneuvering and
outflanking what may be the weakest foreign policy
team in any American administration in the second
half of the century.*

The sanctions regime is indeed collapsing, along with American
policy toward Iraq. In fact, there is little to distinguish the Iraq
sanctions from American policy since American policy is nothing
more than the desperate embrace of sanctions of diminishing
effectiveness punctuated by occasional whining, frequent bluster,
political retreat and military paralysis. What the Administration
calls a policy of containment has become an embarrassment as
our friends and allies in the region and elsewhere ignore our feck-
less imprecations and reposition themselves for Saddam's triumph
over the United States.

INEFFECTIVE POLICY

More than six years after his defeat in Desert Storm, Saddam
Hussein is outsmarting, outmaneuvering and outflanking what
may be the weakest foreign policy team in any American administration in the second half of the century. The coalition once
arrayed against Saddam is in disarray, marking a stunning reversal
of the position of leadership occupied by the United States just six
years ago.

Ambassador Pickering will undoubtedly tell you everything is
fine, that American diplomacy in the Gulf is determined and
effective, that we have been and will continue to be successful in
"containing" Saddam.

But everything isn't fine; American diplomacy in the Gulf is
weak and ineffective; we have been failing to contain Saddam
politically; and he is getting stronger as American policy becomes
manifestly weaker. The United States, mass-marketer to the world,
is losing a propaganda war with Saddam Hussein, mass-murderer
of his own citizens, over the issue of humanitarian concern. With
much of the world believing that Iraqi babies are starving because
of U.S. policies rather than the policies of Saddam Hussein, we
are facing a political-diplomatic defeat of historic significance in
the Gulf, and the Administration, bereft of ideas, energy or imagination, is doing nothing to stop it.

DEFYING SANCTIONS

You will hear from others, perhaps in classified meetings as well as this one, about violations of the existing sanctions against Iraq. I am sure that even the CIA, which has a nearly unbroken record of failure in assessing, understanding and operating in the Gulf, will report how Iraqi oil is loaded on barges and shipped to United Arab Emirates (UAE) waters where, after appropriate fees have been collected by Iran, the cash flows back to Saddam. You will certainly hear about how enough South Korean four-wheel drive vehicles to equip two Republican Guard brigades made it easily through the barriers erected to enforce the current sanctions – barriers, by the way, based on 151 United Nations inspectors overseeing a country of 22 million people. The Committees will learn how Saddam controls the ration cards that tighten his grip on a hapless Iraqi people as they queue up to receive humanitarian food supplies purchased with "oil for food" dollars.

After you have been briefed by the Administration and its experts, after you have examined the facts about the efficacy of the current sanctions and the prospects that they can be kept in place and made effective, I suspect you will come to the following ten conclusions, which I urge you to consider:

SOLUTIONS

First, there is no reason to believe that a continuation of the sanctions will drive Saddam Hussein from power in Iraq or that they will be effective in eliminating his relentless pursuit of weapons of mass destruction.

Second, the pressure to relax the sanctions, which has already pushed to more than ten billion dollars per year the amount of revenue Iraq is allowed from the sale of oil, will not subside and will almost certainly increase.

Third, the French, Russians and others will continue to agitate for the further relaxation of sanctions and the United States will almost certainly make further concessions in this regard.

Fourth, there are already significant violations of the sanctions and these can be expected to continue and even increase. The United Nations is hopelessly ill-equipped to monitor and enforce a strict sanctions regime.

145

Fifth, Saddam's exploitation of the health and hunger issue has created the impression that sanctions, and not Saddam's manipulation of the humanitarian food and medicine programs, is the cause of mass suffering and ill health in Iraq.

Sixth, no one in the region believes that the United States has or will soon adopt a policy that could be effective in bringing Saddam down. The result was a collapse of support for the United States when it blustered about getting tough with Saddam – an inexorable drift away from the U.S. and toward Saddam.

Seventh, when the sanctions have diminished, as they inevitably will, when they have been eroded by circumvention, relaxation and de-legitimization, Saddam's triumph will be complete and he will become the predominant political force in the Gulf region with disastrous consequences for the United States and its allies.

ELIMINATING HUSSEIN

Eighth, Saddam's eventual political victory will be followed by a restoration of his military power.

Ninth, only a policy that is openly based on the need to eliminate the Saddam Hussein regime has any hope of attracting sufficient support in the region to succeed.

Tenth, without legislation and other pressure on the Administration there will be no change in current policy; previous Congressional initiatives will be sidelined or ignored and irreparable damage will be done to the position of the United States in the region and the world.

146

CONTAINING IRAQ: THE COUNTERPOINT

William Blum

William Blum is the author of Killing Hope: U.S. Military and CIA Interventions Since World War II *(Common Courage Press, 1995).*

■ POINTS TO CONSIDER

1. Who does the author hold responsible for the Iraqi-U.S. conflict? Explain.

2. Why does Blum suggest the U.S. allied itself with Iraq?

3. Discuss the ways in which the U.S. aided Iraq's build-up of weapons of mass destruction, according to the article.

4. Summarize the justification the State Department gives for its policy toward Iraq pre-1990.

5. Contrast this reading with the previous reading.

Excerpted from Blum, William. "Anthrax for Export: U.S. Companies Sold Iraq the Ingredients for a Witch's Brew." **The Progressive.** April 1998, 18-20. Reprinted by permission by **The Progressive**, 409 E. Main St., Madison, WI 53703.

American firms supplied Iraq with the specialized hardware vital to the manufacture of nuclear weapons, missiles, and delivery systems.

The United States almost went to war against Iraq in February 1998 because of Saddam Hussein's weapons program. In his State of the Union address, President Clinton castigated Hussein for "developing nuclear, chemical, and biological weapons and the missiles to deliver them."

"You cannot defy the will of the world," the President proclaimed. "You have used weapons of mass destruction before. We are determined to deny you the capacity to use them again."

U.S. BACKED REGIME

Most Americans listening to the President did not know that the United States supplied Iraq with much of the raw material for creating a chemical and biological warfare program. Nor did the media report that U.S. companies sold Iraq more than one billion dollars worth of the components needed to build nuclear weapons and diverse types of missiles, including the infamous Scud....

From 1980 to 1988, Iraq and Iran waged a terrible war against each other, a war that might not have begun if President Jimmy Carter had not given the Iraqis a green light to attack Iran, in response to repeated provocations. Throughout much of the war, the United States provided military aid and intelligence information to both sides, hoping that each would inflict severe damage on the other.

OIL SUPPLY

Noam Chomsky suggests that this strategy is a way for America to keep control of its oil supply:

"It's been a leading, driving doctrine of U.S. foreign policy since the 1940s that the vast and unparalleled energy resources of the Gulf region will be effectively dominated by the United States and its clients, and, crucially, that no independent indigenous force will be permitted to have a substantial influence on the administration of oil production and price."

BIO-WAR

During the Iran-Iraq war, Iraq received the lion's share of American support because at the time Iran was regarded as the greater threat to U.S. interests. According to a 1994 Senate report, private American suppliers, licensed by the U.S. Department of Commerce, exported a witch's brew of biological and chemical materials to Iraq from 1985 through 1989. Among the biological materials, which often produce slow, agonizing death, were:

- *Bacillus anthracis,* cause of anthrax
- *Clostridium botulinum,* a source of botulinum toxin
- *Histoplasma capsulatam,* cause of a disease attacking lungs, brain, spinal cord, and heart
- *Brucella melitensis,* a bacteria that can damage major organs
- *Clostridium perfringens,* a highly toxic bacteria causing systemic illness
- *Clostridium tetani,* a highly toxigenic substance

Also on the list: *Escherichia coli* (E. coli), genetic materials, human and bacterial DNA, and dozens of other pathogenic biological agents. "These biological materials were not attenuated or weakened and were capable of reproduction," the Senate report stated. "It was later learned that these microorganisms exported by the United States were identical to those the United Nations inspectors found and removed from the Iraqi biological warfare program."

The report noted further that U.S. exports to Iraq included the precursors to chemical warfare agents, plans for chemical and biological warfare production facilities, and chemical warhead-filling equipment.

The exports continued till at least November 28, 1989, despite evidence that Iraq was engaging in chemical and biological warfare against Iranians and Kurds since as early as 1984.

The American company that provided the most biological materials to Iraq in the 1980s was American Type Culture Collection (ATCC) of Maryland and Virginia, which made seventy shipments of the anthrax-causing germ and other pathogenic agents, according to a 1996 *Newsday* story....

GULF WAR SYNDROME

In 1994, a group of twenty-six veterans, suffering from what has come to be known as Gulf War Syndrome, filed a billion-dollar lawsuit in Houston against Fisher, Rhone-Poulenc, Bechtel Group, and Lummus Crest, as well as ATCC and six other firms, for helping Iraq to obtain or produce the compounds which the veterans blamed for their illnesses. By 1998, the number of plaintiffs has risen to more than 4,000 and the suit is still pending in Texas.

A Pentagon study in 1994 dismissed links between chemical and biological weapons and Gulf War Syndrome. *Newsday* later disclosed, however, that the man who headed the study, Nobel Laureate Joshua Lederberg, was a director of ATCC. Moreover, at the time of ATCC's shipments to Iraq, which the Commerce Department approved, the firm's CEO was a member of the Commerce Department's Technical Advisory Committee, the paper found.

TECHNICAL KNOW-HOW

A larger number of American firms supplied Iraq with the specialized computers, lasers, testing and analyzing equipment, and other instruments and hardware vital to the manufacture of nuclear weapons, missiles, and delivery systems. Computers, in particular, play a key role in nuclear weapons development. Advanced computers make it feasible to avoid carrying out nuclear test explosions, thus preserving the program's secrecy....

Some of the companies said later that they had no idea Iraq might ever put their products to military use. A spokesperson for Hewlett Packard said the company believed that the Iraqi recipient of its shipments, Saad 16, was an institution of higher learning. In fact, in 1990 *The Wall Street Journal* described Saad 16 as "a heavily fortified, state-of-the-art complex for aircraft construction, missile design, and, almost certainly, nuclear-weapons research."

Other corporations recognized the military potential of their goods but considered it the government's job to worry about it. "Every once in a while you kind of wonder when you sell something to a certain country," said Robert Finney, president of Electronic Associates, Inc., which supplied Saad 16 with a powerful computer that could be used for missile testing and development. "But it's not up to us to make foreign policy," Finney told *The Wall Street Journal*.

U.S. APPROVAL

In 1982, the Reagan Administration took Iraq off its list of countries alleged to sponsor terrorism, making it eligible to receive high-tech items generally denied to those on the list. Conventional military sales began in December of that year. Representative Samuel Gejdenson, Democrat of Connecticut, chairman of a House subcommittee investigating "United States Exports of Sensitive Technology to Iraq," stated in 1991:

"From 1985 to 1990, the United States Government approved 771 licenses for the export to Iraq of $1.5 billion worth of biological agents and high-tech equipment with military application. [Only thirty-nine applications were rejected.] The United States spent virtually an entire decade making sure that Saddam Hussein had almost whatever he wanted...The Administration has never acknowledged that it took this course of action, nor has it explained why it did so. In reviewing documents and press accounts, and interviewing knowledgeable sources, it becomes clear that United States export-control policy was directed by U.S. foreign policy as formulated by the State Department, and it was U.S. foreign policy to assist the regime of Saddam Hussein."

WARNING SIGNS

Subsequently, Representative John Dingell, Democrat of Michigan, investigated the Department of Energy (DOE) concerning an unheeded 1989 warning about Iraq's nuclear weapons program. In 1992, he accused the DOE of punishing employees who raised the alarm and rewarding those who didn't take it seriously. One DOE scientist, interviewed by Dingell's Energy and Commerce Committee, was especially conscientious about the mission of the nuclear nonproliferation program. For his efforts, he received very little cooperation, inadequate staff, and was finally forced to quit in frustration. "It was impossible to do a good job," said William Emel. His immediate manager, who tried to get the proliferation program fully staffed, was chastened by management and removed from his position. Emel was hounded by the DOE at his new job as well.

Another Senate committee, investigating "United States Export Policy Toward Iraq Prior to Iraq's Invasion of Kuwait," heard testimony in 1992 that Commerce Department personnel "changed information on sixty-eight licenses; that references to military end uses were deleted and the designation 'military truck' was

© 1998 Joel Pett, **Lexington Herald-Leader.**

changed. This was done on licenses having a total value of over one billion dollars." Testimony made it clear that the White House was "involved" in "a deliberate effort...to alter these documents and mislead the Congress."

WHY PUNISH OURSELVES?

American foreign policy makers maintained a cooperative relationship with U.S. corporate interests in the region. In 1985, Marshall Wiley, former U.S. ambassador to Oman, set up the Washington-based U.S.-Iraq Business Forum, which lobbied in Washington on behalf of Iraq to promote U.S. trade with that country. Speaking of the Forum's creation, Wiley later explained, "I went to the State Department and told them what I was planning to do, and they said, 'Fine. It sounds like a good idea.' It was our policy to increase exports to Iraq."

Though the government readily approved most sales to Iraq, officials at Defense and Commerce clashed over some of them (with the State Department and the White House backing Commerce).

"If an item was in dispute, my attitude was if they were readily available from other markets, I didn't see why we should deprive American markets," explained Richard Murphy in 1990. Murphy was Assistant Secretary of State for Near Eastern and South Asian Affairs from 1983 to 1989.

SICK SOLDIERS, HEALTHY CORPORATIONS

As it turned out, Iraq did not use any chemical or biological weapons against U.S. forces in the Gulf War. But American planes bombed chemical and biological weapons storage facilities with abandon, potentially dooming tens of thousands of American soldiers to lives of prolonged and permanent agony, and an unknown number of Iraqis to a similar fate. Among the symptoms reported by the affected soldiers are memory loss, scarred lungs, chronic fatigue, severe headache, raspy voice, and passing out. The Pentagon estimates that nearly 100,000 American soldiers were exposed to sarin gas alone.

After the war, White House and Defense Department officials tried their best to deny that Gulf War Syndrome had anything to do with the bombings. The suffering of soldiers was not their overriding concern. The top concerns of the Bush and Clinton Administrations were to protect perceived U.S. interests in the Middle East, and to ensure that American corporations still had healthy balance sheets.

WHAT IS POLITICAL BIAS?

This activity may be used as an individualized study guide for students in libraries and resource centers or as a discussion catalyst in small group and classroom discussions.

Many readers are unaware that written material usually expresses an opinion or bias. The skill to read with insight and understanding requires the ability to detect different kinds of bias. Political bias, race bias, sex bias, ethnocentric bias and religious bias are five basic kinds of opinions expressed in editorials and literature that attempt to persuade. This activity will focus on political bias defined in the glossary below.

Five Kinds of Editorial Opinion or Bias

Sex Bias — The expression of dislike for and/or feeling of superiority over a person because of gender or sexual preference.

Race Bias — The expression of dislike for and/or feeling of superiority over a racial group.

Ethnocentric Bias — The expression of a belief that one's own group, race, religion, culture, or nation is superior. Ethnocentric persons judge others by their own standards and values.

Political Bias — The expression of political opinions and attitudes about government-related issues on the local, state, national or international level.

Religious Bias — The expression of a religious belief or attitude.

154

Guidelines

Read through the following statements and decide which ones represent **political opinion** or **bias.** Evaluate each statement by using the method indicated below.

- **Mark (P)** *for statements that reflect any political opinion or bias.*
- **Mark (F)** *for any factual statements.*
- **Mark (N)** *for any statements that you are not sure about.*

_____ 1. The conflict with Iraq originated because of U.S. complicity in Iraq's build-up of weapons of mass destruction.

_____ 2. The U.S. intervenes intrusively throughout the world. Terrorist attacks against U.S. facilities abroad are expected.

_____ 3. The U.S./Iraqi conflict began in 1990.

_____ 4. Governments must do everything possible to promote democracy and eliminate terrorists.

_____ 5. The U.S. has a successful structure in place to prevent weapons and technology smuggling.

_____ 6. Arms and technology industries pursue sales to questionable countries.

_____ 7. Iraq is still a threat to the U.S.

_____ 8. Saddam Hussein remains a threat to the U.S. because of the inability of its military to effectively stop him.

_____ 9. Companies based in western countries, including the United States, sold vital weapons technology to Iraq.

_____10. Iraq threatens Israeli security.

_____11. Saddam Hussein hides his remaining weapons of mass destruction from the UN inspectors or UNSCOM.

_____12. The U.S. is concerned more with selling goods than with promoting freedom and democracy.

_____13. Russian uranium and weapons stockpiles are ill-secured.

_____14. Osama bin Ladin is the son of a wealthy Saudi.

_____15. Sanctions fueled rather than terminated the Iraqi conflict.

BIBLIOGRAPHY

Book References

Bottome, Edgar M. **The Balance of Terror: Nuclear Weapons and the Illusion of Security.** Boston: Beacon Press, 1986.

Burrows, William E. **Critical Mass: The Dangerous Race for Superpower in a Fragmenting World.** New York: Simon and Schuster, 1994.

Carus, W. Seth. **The Threat of Bioterrorism.** Washington, D.C.: National Defense University, Institute for National Strategic Studies, 1997.

Clark, Ramsey. **Challenge to Genocide: Let Iraq Live.** New York: International Action Center, 1998.

Cole, Leonard A. **The Eleventh Plague: The Politics of Biological and Chemical Warfare.** New York: W.H. Freeman, 1997.

Crime and Political Economy. ed. Ian Taylor. Brookfield, VT: Ashgate, 1998.

Falkenrath, Richard A. **America's Achilles' Heel: Nuclear, Biological and Chemical Terrorism and Covert Attack.** Cambridge, MA: MIT Press, 1998.

Forsberg, Randall. **Nonproliferation Primer: Preventing the Spread of Nuclear, Chemical and Biological Weapons.** Cambridge, MA: MIT Press, 1995.

Geller, Daniel S. **Nations at War: A Scientific Study of International Conflict.** New York: Cambridge University Press, 1998.

Hagerty, Devin T. **The Consequences of Nuclear Proliferation: Lessons from South Asia.** Cambridge, MA: MIT Press, 1998.

Jones, Daniel H. **Implementing the Chemical Weapons Convention: Requirements and Evolving Technologies.** Santa Monica, CA: RAND, 1995.

Kovel, Joel. **Against the State Nuclear Terror.** Boston: South End Press, 1984.

Mauroni, Albert J. **Chemical and Biological Defense: U.S. Military Policies and Decisions in the Gulf War.** Westport, CT: Praeger, 1998.

Mozley, Robert. **The Politics and Technology of Nuclear Proliferation.** Seattle: University of Washington Press, 1998.

NPT, The Non-Proliferation Treaty. Washington, D.C.: ACDA, 1995.

Non-Conventional-Weapons Proliferation in the Middle East: Tackling the Spread of Nuclear, Chemical and Biological Capabilities. ed. Efraim Karsh et al. New York: Oxford University Press, 1993.

Purver, Ron. **Chemical and Biological Terrorism: New Target Threat to Public Safety**. London: Research Institute for the Study of Conflict and Terrorism, 1997.

Spiers, Edward M. **Chemical and Biological Weapons: A Study of Proliferation.** New York: St. Martin's Press, 1994.

Strengthening the Biological Weapons Convention. ed. Erhard Geissler. New York: Oxford University Press, 1990.

Weapons Proliferation in the 1990s. ed. Brad Roberts. Cambridge, MA: MIT Press, 1995.

Journal References

Aizenman, Nurith. "National Security for Sale." **Washington Monthly.** December 1997.

Albright, David, et al. "A Flash from the Past." **Bulletin of Atomic Scientists.** November/December 1997.

Albright, Madeleine K. "A Diplomatic Framework Guiding U.S. Efforts on Nonproliferation." **U.S. Department of State Dispatch.** June 1998.

Annin, Peter and Tom Morganthau. "A Scare in the West." **Newsweek.** March 2, 1998.

Arostegui, Martin. "Fidel Castro's Deadly Secret." **Insight on the News.** July 20, 1998.

"As the War with Terrorists Heats Up, Many Experts Believe Manhattan Could Be Ground Zero." **New York.** November 16, 1998.

Barry, John. "Future Shock." **Newsweek.** July 24, 1995.

Berson, Tom. "Are We Ready for Chemical Warfare?" **Insight on the News.** September 22, 1997.

Braet, Johan, et al. "Plutonium Stockpiles: Searching for Solutions." **Nuclear Engineering International.** October 31, 1998.

"British Fears Over Anthrax." **Maclean's.** April 6, 1998.

Carter, Ashton, et al. "Catastrophic Terrorism." **Foreign Affairs.** November 1998.

Conniff, Ruth. "Proliferation Tango." **The Progressive.** April 1998.

"Danger Zone." **Newsweek.** May 25, 1998.

Dettmer, Jamie. "White House Undercuts Own Nuclear Policy." **Insight on the News.** June 8, 1998.

Foer, Franklin. "Toxic Shock." **The New Republic.** March 16, 1998.

Gaffney, Frank J., Jr. "Making the World Safe for VX." **Commentary.** October 1998.

Gray, Malcolm and William Lowther. "The 'Loose Nukes'." **Maclean's.** April 22, 1996.

Greenfield, Meg. "Not Just a Diversion." **Newsweek.** June 15, 1998.

Guterman, Lila. "Death in the Air." **New Scientist.** September 19, 1998.

Heilbrunn, Jacob. "Playing Defense." **The New Republic.** August 24, 1998.

Hughes, David. "Uranium Seizures Heighten Terrorism Concerns." **Aviation Week and Space Technology.** April 3, 1995.

Hughes, David. "When Terrorists Go Nuclear." **Popular Mechanics.** January 1996.

Istock, Conrad A. "Bad Medicine: Anthrax Vaccinations of U.S.Troops Send a Politically Explosive Message." **Bulletin of the Atomic Scientists.** November/ December 1998.

Jones, Suzanne, et al. "The Question of Pure-Fusion Explosions Under the CTBT." **Physics Today.** September 1998.

Kamp, Karl-Heinz. "An Overrated Nightmare." **Bulletin of the Atomic Scientists.** July/ August 1996.

Katz Keating, Susan. "We Lost New York Today." **The American Legion.** June 1997.

Leifer, John. "Apocalypse Ahead." **Washington Monthly.** November 1997.

McGregor, Alan. "GENEVA: Slow Progress Made on Control of Biological Weapons." **The Lancet.** July 18, 1998.

Moore, Mike. "Nine Minutes to Midnight." **Bulletin of the Atomic Scientists.** September/October 1998.

Nuckolls, John H. "Post-Cold War Nuclear Dangers: Proliferation and Terrorism." **Science.** February 24, 1995.

Paige, Sean. "At the Eleventh Hour." **Insight on the News.** January 26, 1998.

"Reaction Teams Take Up Posts Across USA Against Potential CBW Strikes." **Jane's Defense Weekly.** October 7, 1998.

Rouvray, Dennis H. "The Plague Makers: The Secret World of Biological Warfare." **Chemistry and Industry.** September 7, 1998.

Simon, Jeffrey D. "Biological Terrorism: Preparing to Meet the Threat." **The Journal of the American Medical Association.** August 6, 1997.

Simon, Jeffrey D. "Target U.S.A." **Washington Monthly.** November 1998.

Stein, Jeff. "Praise the Lord and Pass the Anthrax." **Gentlemen's Quarterly.** August 1998.

Timmerman, Tim, et al. "Critical Mass: In the New Nuclear Age, the Rules Aren't Written and Players Are Unpredictable." **U.S. News and World Report.** April 17, 1995.

"To Ban the Bomb." **The Economist.** August 27, 1994.

Travis, John. "New Clue Hints at How Anthrax Kills." **Science News.** May 9, 1998.

Tucker, Jonathan B. "National Health and Medical Services Response to Incidents of Chemical and Biological Terrorism." **Journal of the American Medical Association.** August 6, 1997.

Waller, Douglas. "Nuclear Ninjas." **Time.** January 8, 1996.

Weinberger, Casper. "The Nuclear Proliferation Genie Is Out of the Bottle." **Forbes.** July 6, 1998.

Wilkie, Tom. "Terrorists and the Bomb." **World Press Review.** September 1996.

Wright, Robert. "Be Very Afraid: Nukes, Nerve Gas and Anthrax Spores." **The New Republic.** May 1, 1995.

Wu, Corinna. "Assembling an Antidote to Anthrax." **Science News.** September 5, 1998.

INDEX